decorating basics

Styles · Colors · Furnishings

Better Homes and Gardens® Books
Des Moines, Iowa

Better Homes and Gardens® Books
An imprint of Meredith® Books

Decorating Basics
Editor: Linda Hallam
Design: The Design Office of Jerry J. Rank
Contributing Editors: Susan Andrews, Lynn McBride, Hilary Rose
Copy Chief: Terri Fredrickson
Managers, Book Production: Pam Kvitne, Marjorie J. Schenkelberg
Contributing Copy Editor: Jane Woychick
Contributing Proofreaders: Maria Duryee, Kenya McCullum, Carolyn Petersen
Indexer: Kathleen Poole
Electronic Production Coordinator: Paula Forest
Editorial and Design Assistants: Kaye Chabot, Mary Lee Gavin, Karen Schirm

Meredith® Books
Editor in Chief: James D. Blume
Design Director: Matt Strelecki
Managing Editor: Gregory H. Kayko
Executive Shelter Editor: Denise L. Caringer

Director, Retail Sales and Marketing: Terry Unsworth
Director, Sales, Special Markets: Rita McMullen
Director, Sales, Premiums: Michael A. Peterson
Director, Sales, Retail: Tom Wierzbicki
Director, Book Marketing: Brad Elmitt
Director, Operations: George A. Susral
Director, Production: Douglas M. Johnston

Vice President, General Manager: Jamie L. Martin

Better Homes and Gardens® Magazine
Editor in Chief: Jean LemMon
Executive Interior Design Editor: Sandra S. Soria

Meredith Publishing Group
President, Publishing Group: Stephen M. Lacy
Vice President, Finance and Administration: Max Runciman

Meredith Corporation
Chairman and Chief Executive Officer: William T. Kerr

Chairman of the Executive Committee: E. T. Meredith III

Cover Photograph: Eric Roth

contents

getting started

Decorating is individual and often eclectic, combining the best of styles, periods, patterns, and art to create personal, inviting homes. Although space, style, budget, color, and furnishings all play a role, **decorating is about expressing yourself and living with what you love.** The joy—as well as the challenge—of early 21st century decorating is to learn how to pair elements harmoniously and gracefully. **It's about working with and enjoying** your favorite colors, furnishings, collections, and art. **That's the basics of decorating, and the theme of this book.** Consider decorating a continuing adventure rather than a task to be accomplished. Experienced, professional designers maintain that **well-decorated rooms are never truly finished**—they evolve over time as families and lifestyles change. **The objective of decorating is to create comfortably inviting rooms** that accommodate **your family's lifestyle.** Use the home tours, advice, lessons, color schemes, decorating tips, and sources in this book as tools to help you achieve your individual decorating style. To make decorating a room, or your entire home, as enjoyable and achievable as possible, **this book is divided into five easy-to-read sections.** In the first section, "Find Your Style," tour **the homes of decorating enthusiasts** around the country who share styles, palettes,

budget-stretching tips, and most important—their inspirational stories. **Experience current stylish interpretations and trends,** from updated traditional to mid-20th century modern, rather than strict period re-creations. **You'll learn how** to use color and paint, inexpensive yet effective decorating tools, to infuse your

rooms with your personality. **Every home tour includes starting points,** guidance for selecting colors and fabrics to create a personal look, practical collecting and decorating tips, and distinguishing room details. Turn to the second section of the book, beginning on page 66, **for design school lessons and applicable solutions** based on advice from leading designers and savvy decorating enthusiasts. **With the color chapter** as anchor, you'll build your plan layer by layer—working with fabrics and patterns, windows and walls, and furnishings and floor plans. **Each chapter includes advice,** such as how to work with furniture proportions and room scale, and how to group collections. As the guesswork is eliminated, you'll gain confidence to create your personal eclectic style. **Refer to the Quick Decorating Tips** on pages 112, 136, and 158 for making the most of art with mats and frames, combining fabrics and colors for a unified scheme, and changing the look and style of lamps with updated shades.

findyourstyle

TranslatingTraditional

In North America, traditional style broadly encompasses 18th- and 19th-century furniture and home decorating accessories.

BRITISH FURNITURE AND AMERICAN FURNITURE ARE THE CLASSIC ANCHORS OF THE STYLE; HOWEVER, TRADITIONAL STYLE ALSO INCLUDES FRENCH, SCANDINAVIAN, AND OTHER EUROPEAN FURNITURE. Broad design trends swept through Europe and North America in the late 18th and early 19th centuries, causing similar styles to become popular, but known by different names, in several countries. However, country pieces made of native woods by local craftspeople in Europe and North America were unique to their homelands.

Reproductions and interpretations of traditional furniture styles have been staples of British and American design since the late 19th century. In 1876 in the United States, the American centennial kicked off the craze for colonial-era furniture. Vast quantities of American traditional-style pieces were manufactured during the booming 1920s and remain easy to find at secondhand furniture and antiques stores. Well-known American-manufactured reproduction pieces made after World War II are reliable buys in consignment and thrift shops.

Art, accessories, and collections are important elements in creating a traditional decor. Rugs, porcelains, art pottery, and artifacts from the Near and Far East, India, Africa, and Latin America add personality to the landscapes, still life paintings, and sporting prints that are typical of traditional style. With personal decorating at its height, traditional style is interpreted to fit diverse looks and personal preferences. Accessories and window treatments are pared down and colors are lightened to create youthful, airy versions of this beloved decorating classic. Traditional is a forgiving style. You can introduce a range of styles and periods—including contemporary lighting, fabrics, accent pieces, and art—by pairing pieces of similar proportion and scale.

TRADITIONAL WORKS FOR ELIZABETH. A first-time homeowner, Elizabeth Betts purchased a Nashville, Tennessee, cottage built in the 1940s. The house features traditional elements often lacking in new houses in the same price range. Elizabeth already owned both formal and country-style traditional family pieces, and she collects drawings and maps. Traditional style incorporates these pieces and allows Elizabeth to create a youthful look, *above*.

WOULD TRADITIONAL WORK FOR YOU? Variations of the style work well for all sizes of houses and apartments that were built directly before or after World War II and that have decorative trim and detailing. Traditional also works if you have inherited antiques or family treasures, including vintage reproduction pieces.

EASY STARTING POINTS. If you already own one or two antique, vintage, or reproduction pieces, such as a sofa or chest, use them to anchor your decorating. If you're starting from scratch, look at classic traditional shapes, such as the camelback sofa or classic dining chairs. Feasible starting points are a painting, prints, or collectibles, such as vintage maps or porcelains. **BUDGET STRETCHER:** Start with a sturdy, woven wool kilim rug from a rug store or department store to introduce color and pattern at a fraction of the cost of a true Oriental rug.

ELIZABETH'S STARTING POINTS. During years of apartment living, Elizabeth acquired traditional furnishings, notably a pair of classic reproduction English wing chairs made in the United States. Elizabeth's mother gave her a distinguished family piece, a French-inspired American Empire sofa, *above,* that anchors her living room.

STYLE MAKERS. Classic traditional shapes and styles—such as camelback, Empire, or rolled-arm sofas; wing chairs; or Chippendale, Queen Anne, or Sheraton-style dining chairs—set the look. Turned or barley-twist table legs, dark woods in mahogany or cherry, skirted tables, needlepoint or Oriental rugs, and crystal and silver accessories contribute to the finished setting. Framed mirrors (especially vintage or antique), decorative picture frames, landscapes, still lifes, portrait paintings, and architectural or sporting prints enrich the setting. Well-known traditional style is illustrated by English country houses that are layered with furniture, art, and artifacts contributed by family members throughout the years. Feel confident in mixing pieces from different countries and eras.

BUDGET STRETCHER: Purchase an economical velvet-bound sisal rug for a neat, polished touch. Room-size versions are good buys at under $500.

ELIZABETH'S STYLE MAKERS. A young homeowner on a budget, Elizabeth freely mixes furniture styles and degrees of formality. The country-style cupboard made in Tennessee, *below left,* is highly prized for its regional craftsmanship and relaxes the formality of the Empire sofa and wing chairs. The Empire sofa, *opposite,* is the true star of the living room, working well in the cottage-size home because of its small scale and less ornate detailing. Often overlooked in favor of better-known camelback sofas, Empire pieces, including country-made farm pieces, can be surprisingly good buys.

BUDGET STRETCHER: Don't discount inherited or purchased furniture because of dated or worn upholstery fabrics (traditional dark velvets or silks). You can re-cover the individual pieces to give them renewed life in your home.

COLORS AND FABRICS. Although it's possible to achieve historically correct paint colors for specific eras of architecture and furniture styles, the trend is toward a relaxed interpretation of traditional styles. Designers often use rugs to choose wall colors that match or blend with the major investment. Begin decorating with existing upholstery or draperies, for example, as logical starting points. Appropriate color palettes are serene neutrals—creams, whites, pale taupes; clear pronounced colors such as apple green, icy blue, medium lavender; or deep rich jewel color tones. Rich red, for example, is often used for dining rooms, dens, and libraries. Designers who work with traditional furnishings may advocate painting walls a clear yellow or pink because these colors make attractive backdrops for dark wood furniture and silver accessories.

Natural cottons, linens, silks, and wools or natural fibers (blended with synthetics for durability) lend themselves to traditional settings. Toile scenic prints, authentic plaids of Scottish clans, stripes, and flat woven patterns (such as damask) contribute to the style. Florals, with cream or soft white backgrounds, are handsome with vintage-style furniture. If you are reluctant to decorate with quantities of patterned fabrics, introduce small touches in living room pillows or table skirts. Fabric outlets have good selections of fabrics (see sources on page 160), or substitute mattress ticking or cotton duck for expensive upholstery fabrics. Burlap is useful for stylish and inexpensive window treatments.

ELIZABETH'S PALETTE AND PATTERNS. Elizabeth prefers neutrals with punches of color and pattern. She retained the kitchen's bright yellow laminate backsplash, *opposite left,* freshening the cabinets, shelves, and trim with bright white paint and the wall with soft gray paint. She chose two different toiles—the perennially popular classic French scenic fabric—for her decorating. A tan and black toile is used in the fabric-saving Roman shades that finish the living room, *page 12.* A toile on the dining room windows and chair seats coordinates with the raspberry plaid clip-on shades that update the small chandelier, *above center.* In lieu of a headboard, Elizabeth used the fabric-softened shuttered window and an architectural fragment to frame the bed, *above right.*

ELIZABETH'S FINISHING TOUCHES. Emulating the style of grand old Tennessee houses, black baseboards, *opposite,* contrast with the kitchen's freshly painted white trim. Rather than remove the wall-mounted mirror over the mantel, *page 11,* Elizabeth refined it with mitered molding and leaned a small framed mirror against the backdrop. For the dining room and bedroom, Elizabeth introduced symmetry and order with pairs of identically framed and matted photographs and prints respectively, *above center* and *above right.*

The Art of Color

Bold art and colorful walls work harmoniously together when you choose hues that flatter your artwork.

FOR WALL COLORS, CHOOSE SHADES AND FINISHES THAT ENHANCE AND FRAME PAINTINGS, PRINTS, OR POSTERS WITHOUT OVERPOWERING THEM. Select neutral fabrics for furnishings and minimize accessories. For dedicated art collectors, the presentation of the artwork is of paramount importance. Although the pristine gallery-like quality of white or pale neutral walls has undisputed appeal, color devotees can select shades that enrich their acquisitions. Confidence and a willingness to experiment will achieve the most flattering shades for your walls. Contributing to the look is the discipline to focus on art and to resist filling rooms with fabric patterns and an abundance of accessories and collectibles.

A COLORFUL PALETTE WORKS FOR MARY.

Dramatic paint colors have always been an economical way for Mary O'Brien and her husband, Dennis, of Chicago to stamp individuality on their homes. After she painted the dingy off-white living room in her first apartment a dramatic navy blue, Mary was convinced of the power of color. As her art interests evolved, she gravitated toward bold paintings, lithographs, and etchings that stand out against blue and red walls. Mary carefully works with painters to custom mix paint, which allows her to create shades that work for the exposure, lighting, and art in each room. She gives extra attention to backdrops by ragging and stippling the walls.

WOULD DECORATING WITH COLOR AND ART WORK FOR YOU?

If you love art and vibrant, colorful walls, use them to maximize your decorating options. For the most impact, use neutral, unpatterned fabrics for major upholstered pieces, plain materials—such as glass or acrylic—for coffee or side tables, simple window treatments, and carefully edited accessories. Color and art become the interior stars; fabric and furnishings are supporting players.

EASY STARTING POINTS. The classic starting points of art—paintings, prints, or posters—work especially well in rooms with little color or pattern in the furnishings. Create a color palette by pulling a pale, soft, or neutral shade from the art. A bolder method, which Mary advocates, is to base the scheme on the most arresting color.

Designers often recommend basing a color scheme on a rug. Because rugs are major investment pieces and finding a rug to work with existing painted walls is challenging, it is easier to coordinate the wall color to the rug. If you prefer pattern and color in upholstered pieces, window treatments, or accent pillows, fabric can be an ideal origin of a room's color palette. Collectors also base schemes on colors that flatter their porcelains, pottery, or other treasures.

MARY'S STARTING POINTS. Art—bold paintings, subtle lithographs and etchings, posters—gave Mary the needed color cues. Paintings inspired the deep blue in the living room, *top left* and *top right;* however, Mary and the painter mixed the shade to match the rim on a favorite antique Oriental plate. The dining room, *right* and *opposite,* has a similar story. A small painting in her collection is noted for a red-roofed cottage. The color appeals to Mary, who also found an identical shade—hibiscus red—on the trim of one of her scarves.

MARY'S STYLE MAKERS. Art hung on colorful walls and balanced by white upholstery fabric creates Mary's personal decorating theme. Original and colorful paintings, including thrift store and student sale finds, bestow flair and personality. Mary uses large, bold pieces for scale, with smaller, more subdued pieces for balance.

STYLE MAKERS. When color and art set the tone of your decor, the key to style is the boldness and drama of at least one element. Several large paintings anchor the scheme and balance smaller paintings. When small paintings are used, they gain importance and visual interest when they are stacked and grouped rather than hung solo. Dramatic colorful posters—originals or reproductions—relax the look and add scale. This art-based theme is most successful when other objects, such as plates or collectibles, are not grouped on the wall with paintings.

Mary displays lithographs and etchings to add refinement to her dining room, *page 19*. Black and white art photography and prints, purchased or taken with your own camera, are stylish alternatives that work well with an array of contemporary furnishings and rugs.

MARY'S PERSONAL PALETTE. Mary worked out a personal palette during the years she commuted to her job as a law librarian. To pass the time, she planned her home's ideal look, figuring in time and budget constraints. Her solution was to pair colorful walls with the art she collects and to cover major furniture pieces in economical, washable white cotton duck. Art sets the color schemes for the living and dining rooms, ragged deep blue and hibiscus red, respectively. The honey stripes of the adjacent family room play off the red dining room walls and the wood tones.

Although Mary loves lively color in living and dining areas, she chose white and soft neutrals to create a relaxing sitting room, *above*. White and small patterns update inherited and acquired traditional furniture pieces.

MARY'S FINISHING TOUCHES. Mary edits details to finish and energize her look. A faux zebra chair, *pages 16–17*, punches up the color block scheme of the living room's blue walls and white upholstery. Drapery panels on iron rods soften windows without elaborate or fussy top treatments. Picture lamps call attention to large artwork. Mary varies her framing styles, using wide mats to make smaller artwork more important and interesting. To relax art, she breaks up the symmetry of the mantel arrangement, *page 18,* by casually leaning a small painting against the wall. A violin, carefully placed as art, acknowledges her love of music. She leans, rather than hangs, a striking painting against the wall above the console in the family room, *left*. Mary uses a mix of tabletop and floor lamps to create pleasing reading light and to accommodate visiting.

Fresh '50s Funk

Mid-20th-century design is back in a big way—with lively pieces furnishing homes for another generation of families.

THE POPULAR '50S-STYLE REFERS TO THE MODERN MASS-PRODUCED FURNITURE OF THE POSTWAR ERA. ALTHOUGH MANY FAMILIES KEPT TRADITIONAL FURNISHINGS, they added chrome and vinyl dinette sets in breakfast rooms and stylishly pale, sleek furniture in bedrooms. Until recently, dinette sets from the '50s were thrift store finds; now dinette sets in reasonably good condition are in high demand, which has led to the recent manufacture of reproduction sets and individual chairs. Also during the '50s, vast quantities of accessories—whimsical lamps, mirrors, rugs, and dinnerware—were manufactured to furnish the abundance of newly built houses and apartments. Plain box-style houses of the late '40s were replaced with the low-slung ranch-style homes that are identified with the era. Many variations of the ranch-style home, built all across the country, dominated the housing market until the '60s and '70s.

WHY '50s-STYLE WORKS FOR MATT AND CHRISTI. With a background in art and design, Matt Strelecki gravitated toward Art Deco, the streamlined Art Moderne home furnishings style of the 1920s through the early 1940s. As prices for these sleek furnishings skyrocketed, Matt and his wife, Christi, were increasingly frustrated in their search. Although they continued to look for Art Deco, they noticed the solid shapes and interesting lines of mid-century modern furniture and accessories. The combination of practical and sturdy wood furniture, curvy upholstered pieces, and funky lamps and accessories inspired a new collecting direction. Much more plentiful than Art Deco and relatively affordable, mass-produced mid-century modern continues to attract collectors who appreciate the originality and energy of the postwar years.

Matt enjoys the hunt and the thrill of finding just the right pieces and accessories to furnish their home. He also enjoys working with dealers, researching pieces, and buying and trading pieces to achieve the look he wants. Matt and Christi are patient—willing to wait for the right piece to surface.

Early in their conversion to '50s furnishings, they made a conscious decision to collect Heywood-Wakefield furniture. The solid construction and smooth lines of this birch furniture work well for the family's active household of three young daughters. The curved lines and generous proportions of '50s sofas are comfortable for the family. In addition, they have found a plethora of accessories—including art, fabrics, and rugs—to make collecting fun for the whole family.

WOULD DECORATING WITH '50s FURNISHINGS WORK FOR YOU? You either love it or hate it. From the 1920s to the present, architects and interior designers have worked with sleek contemporary furniture and modern (often abstract) art to create the style widely known as modern or contemporary. Some of the best-known contemporary furniture pieces were designed by European and American architects. What does this mean for the '50s funk fan? If you live in a postwar ranch-style house or apartment, the typical horizontal lines, 8-foot ceilings, and minimal trim work well as the backdrop for '50s furniture, which was originally designed for these spaces. If you live in an older or more traditional house with detailing and trim, consider mixing '50s-style tables with traditional and or more recent contemporary pieces. Collectors aren't able to walk into home furnishings stores and find the complete '50s look. Be willing to work with dealers and to scour shops, tag sales, thrift stores, and the Internet if you plan to completely furnish a home in this artful style.

COLLECTING TIPS. Until recently, '50s fans could find real deals in thrift and consignment stores, on the Internet, and even at tag sales. With the growing popularity of the '50s look, particularly on the East and West Coasts and in major cities, bargains are hard to find, but they are out there for those who search diligently. Specialty home furnishings shops have sprung up to cater to fans. The Internet has also been a boon to collectors, buyers, and sellers. If you live in an area where the popularity of '50s-style hasn't yet returned, investigate thrift and consignment stores first. Also look for pieces at tag sales. Wood and molded plastic furniture is often in excellent condition. Wood pieces may simply need to be cleaned or waxed—or at most, refinished. Be prepared to have upholstered pieces re-covered or even rebuilt. Sofas and chairs were the growing-up furniture of the baby boomer generation. In many cases, the furniture withstood considerable stress.

MATT AND CHRISTI'S COLLECTING TIPS. Their two cardinal rules: Don't buy something just because it is cheap, and don't buy a project. They've found that if they buy a piece in less than usable condition, it stays that way. Matt and Christi also suggest honing in on one style and finish for wood pieces. They collect only the champagne color of the Encore line of Heywood-Wakefield so that they can move pieces from room to room. Heywood-Wakefield works well for

their daughters' rooms because it is sturdy and because twin beds are available.

Matt and Christi recommend that novice collectors start with small, inexpensive pieces—such as coffee tables, side tables, and lamps—and then decide whether the style would appeal on a larger scale. Matt advises buying pieces that you like when you find them; if you don't, they may soon be sold to another devotee of the style. When lamps, chairs, or tables are sold in pairs, Matt buys them. Pairs pull a room together and will be in demand if he decides to trade or sell the pieces later. Matt suggests developing a relationship with a reputable dealer who knows your tastes and styles and who will help you trade pieces.

COLORS AND FABRICS. Bark cloth, the signature fabric of the '50s funk look, is a sturdy woven printed fabric used for draperies. Search for it at secondhand stores that specialize in '50s furnishings; it is also bought and sold on the Internet. Stylized prints tend to include the greens, browns, and blues of the era. Orange, yellow, pink, black, and occasionally red are also associated with '50s-style.

MATT AND CHRISTI'S PERSONAL PALETTE. Because they live in a climate with long winters, Matt and Christi opted for shades of yellow and green for the primary palette. Their goal was to have no white walls in the house. The walls and vaulted ceiling of the living room are painted yellow, *page 23*. The brick hearth, mantel, and cabinets are pale yellow. Yellow and dark brown are used for accent walls adjacent to the room's open entry. Touches of orange and the turquoise blue associated with the '50s enliven rooms throughout the house.

DETAILS THAT COUNT. Matt and Christi found that adding more '50s furnishings unified and strengthened the overall appearance of their home. Some of the window treatments are vintage bark cloth draperies. Abstract patterned area rugs of the era are also used. In addition, vintage fiberglass planters neatly hold the houseplants. Matt gravitates toward lighting fixtures, including characteristic colored glass pendent lights, and he has a particular interest in the space-age lamps designed and manufactured by the Majestic and Luxcraft companies.

One final touch: Matt developed a gallery-type framing system using picture wire and double chrome spa hooks. With picture wire attached to the artwork and spa hooks on every wall, Matt and Christi can easily rotate artwork as they acquire or change pieces.

When Collections Are Key

Dedicated collectors share a passion for acquiring the objects of their desire. Whatever the collection, surfaces should showcase rather than compete with the objects on display.

SPACE WORKS WELL WHEN COLLECTIONS INTEGRATE WITH THE OVERALL DECORATING SCHEME. ROOMS THAT ARE DECORATED AS BACKGROUNDS FOR ART AND FINDS BECOME COMFORTABLE LIVING SPACES, NOT MUSEUMS. Collection-based decorating is stimulated by a genuine interest—a school of painting, a type of pottery, textiles, or decorative objects. Whether the collection is inherited, assembled over the years, or a new interest, it can direct the decorating scheme for a room or an entire home. Personal interest, rather than quantities of objects, is the incentive for collection-based decorating. Color schemes for rooms are often inspired by a favorite pottery piece, a painting, or other art. Collectors and decorators then have the challenge and reward of adding to and refining the growing collection.

WHY COLLECTING WORKS FOR CORT. The grandson of a sea captain who collected during his travels, Cort Sinnes gravitated toward collecting and paintings early in life. Cort acquired his first antique, a mahogany desk, when he was just 15 years old. A watercolorist in his own right, he has had a lifelong interest in California landscapes and abstract art. Cort collects 19th- and early 20th-century California pottery and is intrigued by the work of a contemporary California art potter who works with traditional glazes.

Rather than follow precise design trends, Cort gradually acquires art that agrees with the room's background colors.

WOULD DECORATING WITH COLLECTIONS WORK FOR YOU? If you own or are acquiring a collection, use your acquisitions as the focal point of your decorating and follow a few uncomplicated rules. Don't force your interests simply because you enjoy the appeal of an assembled collection in someone's home. Collect what attracts you. If you relish the

search and acquisition, collect what can reasonably be found in your area or travels. As your knowledge and collections grow, edit out, trade up, and rotate pieces. If one color dominates—such as blue willow or green majolica pottery, for example—choose a decorating palette that enhances your collection. Color intensity and shade affect background color. Choose enough contrast to ensure that backgrounds don't overpower the highlighted collections.

EASY STARTING POINTS. An admired painting, print, poster, quilt, or piece of pottery can set the room's direction. Pull a color from the artwork and use it as a complementary backdrop. At first, work with lighter or neutral shades from the art. For example, if a painting or art poster has shades of cobalt blue, deep sage green, dark red, and warm tan, choose tan or a lighter tint of the green or blue. If you are unsure of which color to paint an art-filled room, go beyond white to warm sand—a shade that designers often use to warm art-filled spaces.

CORT'S STARTING POINTS. The blue tile fireplace surround, *page 28,* sets the scheme. To incorporate the existing tile into the living room, Cort recalled an old magazine photograph of olive drab walls. He experimented with three variations of color before finding the shade that worked best with his artwork. His collection of California

pottery, his inherited furniture, and his watercolors are additional points of departure for his decorating.

ARRANGING TIPS. Group, group, group—rather than scatter—to give collections more importance and interest. Vary the elevations of display objects by using books, stands, boxes, easels, and plate stands. Err on the low side when hanging art. In homes, art is typically viewed from a seated rather than a standing position. Creatively arrange and stack art. Hanging small paintings below a larger one increases the interest of each. Before hanging art, use paper templates to work out arrangements on the floor. Coordinate matting or frames on prints, photos, or small art, and update existing mismatched frames by painting them a single neutral color. Narrow black frames and cream mats are a tasteful, stylish combination. Also factor lighting into art arrangements. Use picture lights, available at home furnishings and lighting stores, to illuminate large artwork.

CORT'S ARRANGING TIPS. Arrange a tabletop and the adjoining wall above it as a collage. Confidently mix art styles; buy art that appeals to you and it will work together. Follow this advice when you consider purchasing art: If you see a piece in a gallery, ask to have the piece held overnight. If you can recall the piece the next day, it's memorable to you and therefore worth purchasing. At a one-day art show or art fair,

DETAILS THAT COUNT. Paired objects and symmetrical arrangements bring order and calm to diverse collections. When purchasing objects such as urns, vases, and small lamps, buy two of each. Unify a room filled with many objects by coordinating frames, mats, and lampshades. Unusual pillows, carefully edited memorabilia, and suitably framed family photographs personalize and warm art-filled rooms.

CORT'S FINISHING TOUCHES. Cort utilizes space in his home by displaying kitchen collectibles on open shelves, *page 33;* hanging art over doorways; and creating a mini art gallery in his bathroom, *opposite*. Throughout his home, touches of black in lampshades and frames add visual weight and accent. Cort introduces the unexpected: Rather than a large painting over the mantel, two small paintings flank a vertical mirror, *page 28*. Favorite paintings and posters become even more significant when illuminated by picture lights; other art leans on easels and stands.

walk away for at least an hour to ensure that the piece truly appeals to you. Purchase an easel to allow for quick changes of art to fit your mood or the season. Display matted and framed art created or collected by you or your family—sketches, photographs, or postcards. Cort paints watercolors on his travels.

COLORS AND FABRICS. Use neutral colors and minimal patterns when collections are the focal point. Choose solids or subtle woven textures; avoid busy florals, plaids, or stripes. Include pillows and throws for seasonal color and warmth.

CORT'S PERSONAL PALETTE. Cort delights in color and has never lived with white walls. He uses dramatic color to define public spaces. To make brilliant color work in his small house, he chose hues of the same intensity. Deep olive walls and white woodwork paired with white slipcovers set the stage in the art-filled living room. (Because Cort shares his home with his pet dog, he relies on washable cotton duck slipcovers.) Cort and his guests enjoy the warm glow of the Chinese red walls in the dining room, *page 32*. Mustard yellow, derived from the California pottery, warms the small kitchen, while the bedroom is a serene shade of pale taupe.

CountryFrenchAmbience

The appeal is understandable—mellow woods, colorful pottery and fabrics, and dressy flourishes exude the warmth and joy of life.

FRENCH INFLUENCE ON AMERICAN DESIGN CONTINUES TO EVOLVE. ALTHOUGH THE HIGH FORMAL STYLES AND SLEEK MID-20TH CENTURY LOOKS HAVE MANY FANS, COUNTRY FRENCH IS BY FAR THE MOST POPULAR IN NORTH AMERICA. This warm and welcoming style combines rustic and refined—featuring the unpolished woods of the French countryside. Pieces in this provincial style are typically pine or fruitwood. Carving, rather than gilding, gives detail to the pieces. Background wall and floor colors tend to be soft and neutral. Fabrics, often in the cheerful yellows, blues, or reds of Provence, are cotton.

Through the years, American designers and people with a fondness for French style have put their individual spin on Country French. The style often incorporates formal pieces of French furniture and art —the type of treasure a French country family might have brought home from the city. American translations, in the melting pot tradition, often include English art and accessories as well as interesting collectibles from other countries.

WHY COUNTRY FRENCH WORKS FOR SUSAN AND JACK. A native of southern Louisiana, where French heritage is valued, Susan Arnold has had a lifelong interest in all things French. Susan is an interior designer, and her shop features French furnishings. She and Jack Arnold, an architect, travel frequently in France for business and pleasure. With their combined creative backgrounds, both

enjoy the personal, eclectic mix of Country French. Because the couple frequently entertains family and friends,. they prefer furnishings and fabrics that stand up to everyday use.

WOULD DECORATING WITH COUNTRY FRENCH WORK FOR YOU? The first prerequisite is the simplest: Do you enjoy French culture and style? If you do, almost any residence that has neutral walls and flooring can take on charming French accents. If you like the mellow tones of unpolished or lightly polished fruitwoods and pine, you'll enjoy Country French. Because furniture stars in this style, you'll need one or two key pieces—such as an armoire, a pair of chairs, or dining chairs—to anchor the look. If you own gently curved armchairs, they can be re-covered in a cotton print for a decidedly French look. Country French works well for decorating enthusiasts who enjoy mixing fabrics and patterns, window treatments, and accessories.

STYLE MAKERS. Of all the popular decorating styles and looks, Country French is the most furniture dependent. A few French-style anchor pieces—not strictly French-made—are needed to convey a provincial flair in a room. Reproduction Country French-style or French-influenced furniture, including sofas and love seats, is widely marketed in a variety of price ranges. Mass market catalog retailers sell furniture with distinctive French accents. Unfinished French-style pieces, including dining chairs, are also available. Whatever their origin, key pieces include carved or painted armoires, bergères (closed-arm armchairs), fauteuils (open-arm armchairs), farm-style dining tables, and dining chairs. Chairs in the French style may have rush seats, another unmistakable style maker.

Glazed and unglazed olive oil jars, pottery, urns, toile (the French scenic print fabric and wallpaper), cafe-style curtains, and lace all contribute to the appealing style.

SUSAN AND JACK'S STYLE MAKERS. Major furniture pieces mixed with funky finds create the couple's Country French look. Among their style setting pieces are an 18th-century French farm table, a fruitwood grandfather clock, a mixture of paired and single French chairs, and an 18th-century mirror from Paris. On the more casual side, Susan added a salvaged chandelier, dressed up with mismatched crystals, and a piano stool that serves as a coffee table.

COLORS AND FABRICS. Soft neutral shades of cream, tan, and off-white work well for Country French interiors. Stone, as well as wood, is appropriate for living area floors. Painted wood and rough cedar add the texture associated with sunny Provence. Patterned or toile wallpaper frequently appears in dining rooms, small sitting rooms, bedrooms, and baths. Cotton prints in the Country French style feature clear shades of blue, yellow, green, and brick red. Although toile, the scenic print, is the fabric associated with French-style decorating, plaids, checks, and floral are sometimes part of

the Americanized mix. Country French rooms usually take on a sophisticated air by mixing neutral taupes, creams, and beiges in textured linens and cottons. However, proponents of more color also create beautiful rooms with the sun-warmed, earthy shades and clear colors of Mediterranean countries. Fabrics tend to be simple and tailored; window treatments include panels hung from iron rods and lace cafe curtains.

SUSAN AND JACK'S PERSONAL PALETTE. Susan and Jack prefer color, texture, and pattern in their rooms. They favor wood floors, which are softened with Oriental rugs, in living areas. Walls are painted a light taupe with off-white trim to offset the richly hued rugs and mixture of vibrant fabrics. Susan envisions color schemes and dominant colors for each room and works from her plan. For major furnishing pieces, she plays with fabric swatches until she achieves a balance

of dominant and supportive patterns. With blue and red as anchor colors, Susan fearlessly mixes fabric patterns in the living and dining areas. She combines large-scale patterns in clear primary colors with open florals, checks, and plaids. For casual areas, she introduces the buttery yellow and red associated with Provence. Susan uses toile as an accent fabric, not as a main player. Rather than a set number of patterns or colors, Susan uses a general rule for each room: Include enough small scale neutral fabrics to balance the visual energy of the space.

DETAILS THAT COUNT. Collections and accessories are important elements of Country French decorating. Olive oil jars, urns, architectural fragments, carved mirrors, distressed finishes, French pottery, and porcelains all contribute to the look.

Color It Contemporary

Blocks of saturated color—painted with the confident touch of an abstract artist—energize sleek contemporary architecture.

BOLD COLOR IS APPLIED SELECTIVELY—PERHAPS TO A WALL OR ON LARGE UNFRAMED CANVASES. MID- TO LATE-20TH-CENTURY DESIGN HAS ITS MINIMAL COLOR DEVOTEES, but some advocates of contemporary style are discovering the joys of color and craft and using them to define and warm open spaces. Like traditional and country and cottage decorating, contemporary design is becoming more personal. If you have a contemporary house or contemporary furniture, you can successfully infuse your home with vibrant color and the creativity of many cultures.

WHY COLORFUL CONTEMPORARY WORKS FOR MARIA AND BRUCE. Maria Stark and Bruce Dobb are drawn to the exuberant, sun-warmed hues of Mexico. Living in California, they readily collect sculptures and paintings from Mexico in order to experience the intriguing culture. Their diverse interests include folk art masks, Fiesta products, and mid-20th century modern furniture, all of which lend vibrant color and strong form to settings. They also collect vintage white California pottery, which visually pops against colorful backdrops. Contrasting color works well for Bruce and Maria because it allows them to define areas within an open floor plan. Color also creates the trim and detailing otherwise lacking in sleek contemporary design.

WOULD COLORFUL CONTEMPORARY WORK FOR YOU? If you like the clean lines of modern architecture and contemporary furniture as well as the energy of saturated colors, this is the style for you. This colorful interpretation of contemporary design works best in gutsy, bold strokes. Color effectively defines spaces in open floor plans when it is applied in broad, contrasting swaths. Although the look is ideal for '50s and '60s ranch houses and later contemporary designs, it translates to traditional homes too. If you have the confidence to work within a traditional-style home to achieve this look, the key is to contrast color from room to room and to furnish sparely with contemporary classics.

EASY STARTING POINTS. Color is the energizing and space-defining element in your decorating scheme. Start with the main living area and work from there to create a room-by-room color plan. For the first room in your scheme, choose the color that most appeals to you. If you've always wanted a red or yellow room—have it. If one color doesn't readily come to mind, use an object from a collection—such as bright pottery, a painting, or a poster—for inspiration. Also look through tile samples and paint chips for appealing colors.

MARIA AND BRUCE'S STARTING POINTS. As proponents of color, Maria and Bruce have multiple personal decorating incentives. The design of their home, with perimeter and interior half-walls, fostered the use of solid hues for the partition and multi-colors for the interior dividers. A photograph in a foods magazine inspired the papaya color that enlivens the dining area. In the kitchen, *page 49,* a lipstick red sink, black tiles, and a Fiesta products collection complement green walls and yellow cabinets. The view of distant hills sparked the concept of using green walls to erase indoor boundaries.

STYLE MAKERS. Maria and Bruce's collection of mid-20th century furniture, including basic mass market pieces found at flea markets and secondhand shops, ties the modern home to the modern sofa, chairs, and tables of the 1950s. Well-known shapes appear in the divided sectional sofa, *opposite and below,* in an amoeba-shape coffee table and canvas butterfly chairs. Selective touches evoke mid-20th century California glamour—for example, the curvy black chair reminiscent of the 1930s, *page 45,* accompanied by a funky white '50s sofa, both covered in synthetic leather. The sofa, trimmed in faux fur, an imitation cheetah pillow and bench, and wall-to-wall zebra-motif carpeting contrast with multi-color walls. Folk art masks, Mexican art, Fiesta products, and California pottery further define the couple's personalities.

PALETTE POINTERS. Bold, saturated colors call for bold strokes. To mix intense colors, for the most dramatic definition effects, think contrast rather than blend. Less saturated colors, with less intense values, appear weak when paired with vibrant clear colors. THE BOTTOM LINE: If you use intense clear red in one room, use an equally intense color in adjoining spaces. Achieve this balanced intensity by choosing paint colors from one manufacturer and from the same position on the paint chip cards (paint chip cards normally range from the lightest to the deepest degree of color). For walls that are in reasonably good condition, consider using semigloss paint to provide depth, dimension, and movement to color-saturated surfaces.

ART AND ACCESSORIES. In addition to their collections of folk art masks and Mexican art, Maria and Bruce collect contemporary poster-size prints. For interest, they mix sizes and framing styles, including unframed art pieces. Recessed lighting, favored in late 20th-century contemporary homes, and funky '50s-style lamps enhance the colorful rooms. The couple adds lighthearted touches—such as playful fake banana palms with parrots, *page 46*. Equally important to the success of the design: They know when to stop adding and start enjoying.

New Country Colonial

Classic American design married with clean, uncluttered living spaces elicits a pared down, airy, contemporary version of Country Colonial.

THIS PERSONAL DESIGN STYLE COMBINES THE BEST OF CLASSIC AMERICAN FURNISHINGS WITH OPEN YET TRADITIONAL SPACES. New Country Colonial has its roots in the farmhouses of the American Colonial era and the early 19th century. The house type most associated with American Colonial style is the center hall plan. Ingenious in its simplicity, this floor plan features rooms opening off the center hall. Typically, the earliest modest center hall houses were one room deep—one room on each side of the hall. Later four or more rooms opened off the center hall. Two- and three-story versions featured a stairwell in the center hall. In cold areas the center hall was narrow and the compact rooms had low-ceilings to retain heat. In warmer climates, the hall widened into a breezeway for air circulation.

This style of decorating melds 18th- and 19th-century furniture and art with contemporary furnishings and neutral backgrounds. When they are used, antiques and reproduction furniture pieces stand out against subdued backgrounds. The objective is to create contemporary living spaces in comfortable, inviting rooms rather than to re-create the past in museum-like settings.

WHY NEW COUNTRY COLONIAL WORKS. With access to New England shops and to flea markets that have antique furnishings, the owners favor 19th-century American farmhouse styles. As the parents of young children and as pet owners, they prefer an open, livable interior style and sturdy furniture designs.

WOULD NEW COUNTRY COLONIAL WORK

FOR YOU? New Country Colonial translates well into traditional and contemporary living spaces. Because the look hinges on the farmhouse quality of New England and East Coast antiques, it becomes a challenge to achieve in more formal settings (such as Tudor-style houses) or in strongly regional styles, Southwestern-style, for example. Simple pieces of New England furnishings—the classic Windsor chair, for instance—may appear out of place and overwhelmed in robust bungalow styles, which are better appointed with Arts and Crafts furnishings.

The style works well if you enjoy 18th- and 19th-century American furnishings associated with New England and the eastern seaboard. The pared-down look is attractive for those who are just beginning to collect or who have the discipline to wait for the right

piece or the opportunity to trade up for key pieces. The look is a natural for families with young children and lively house pets. Delicate accessories are kept to a minimum, and upholstered pieces are chosen for unassuming lines, durability, and comfort. Antiques, such as farm tables and Windsor-style chairs, are sturdy. New Country Colonial is a pleasing compromise for those who are drawn to clean lines but who find a strictly contemporary style too austere. On the downside, avid collectors may feel inhibited by display limitations and the requisite paring down. The subdued backdrops and minimal accessories may appear spartan to proponents of color and pattern.

EASY STARTING POINTS. If you own a piece or two of classic American furniture—antique, vintage, or reproduction—use that as a beginning. Plain upholstered chairs or sofas in classic shapes and neutral materials are solid starters. A painting or collection, such as New England pottery pieces or pewter, are starting points—especially if you are

willing to pare down. Those who are proceeding from scratch should choose light neutral walls and flooring and minimal window treatments.

STYLE MAKERS. Windsor chairs and Country Colonial versions of classic Chippendale-style chairs are ideal beginnings. Well-made reproductions, antiques, or vintage furniture pieces work equally well. In common usage, a true antique is at least 100 years old; vintage refers to pieces that were made before World War II but are less than 100 years old. The term vintage is often used for furniture that was made in the United States and Great Britain during the 1920s. It is often easier to find than pieces from Europe.

Consider pine or rustic farm-style tables for informal dining areas and traditional tables for formal dining rooms. For living areas, accent tables range from tilt-top and pub styles to tripod variations. For upholstered pieces, select well-proportioned

traditional classics, such as rolled-arm and exposed-leg sofas. Current upholstered pieces, such as the wide chair-and-a-half with exaggerated rolled arms, overpower antique-style furnishings. Whether you buy new or re-cover existing chairs or sofas, select neutral or subdued solid fabrics; avoid florals and busy prints. A classic 19th-century piece—a camelback sofa, for example—will blend more attractively in an off-white textured cotton than in a period damask.

Use light neutral backgrounds—painted walls, sisal rugs, tightly looped beige or light taupe carpeting—to contribute to the overall appeal. New England-style collectibles—toys, pewter, weather vanes, lightning rods, clocks, baskets, and quilts—stand out against plain white or off-white backgrounds. Black wrought iron and rustic country-style chandeliers also contrast well with a light backdrop.

PERSONAL STYLE MAKERS. The interplay of neutral walls, classic furniture styles, and minimal accessories brings this look together. A few well-chosen contemporary pieces—including metal chairs that are paired with a formal turned-leg mahogany dining table, *page 52*—update the style without disturbing the serene neutral scheme. Floor lamps add visual interest and give the open floor plan cozy reading areas, *page 55*. Edited accessories are striking: a garden armillary sphere, *page 51,* a metal trunk with nailheads, antique toys, *page 56,* and a child's ladder-back chair. As color and pattern are downplayed, furniture and accessories become design statements.

PALETTE POINTERS. Work with a neutral palette, adding textures and touches of natural, subdued color for interest. Paint walls soft white or off-white, eliminating wallpaper and decorative finishes; add tints and textures in subdued colors. Natural shades—such as moss green, rust, and muted mustard—enliven without jarring the setting. Include wood tones to warm the coolly serene rooms. Use pattern sparingly: Decorate with pillows covered in toned-down stripes or geometric fabrics rather than bold or novelty prints. When window treatments are needed, choose drapery panels, shutters, or shades. Avoid elaborate top treatments and ornate detailing and trims.

SouthwesternSpirited

Warm, earthy desert colors, rough-hewn woods, and handcrafted decorative furnishings of Mexico and the American Southwest characterize a style as lyrical as the wide-open landscape.

THE SOUTHWESTERN LOOK IS CLOSELY IDENTIFIED WITH THE TRADITIONAL ADOBE HOUSES OF THE SOUTHWEST REGION. Native art, artifacts, and cultures of Mexico and the American Southwest—notably the desert tribes—influence the look. Spanish Colonial architecture and Latin American influences also play a role in the style. Artist colonies in Santa Fe and Taos, New Mexico, contribute to popular interest in the region's art, colors, and motifs. Because Southwestern decorating melds cultures and periods, antiques and paintings collected throughout North America are suited to this eclectic mix.

WHY SOUTHWEST WORKS FOR TYLER. Tyler Atkinson lives in Tucson and has convenient access to Mexico. She has restored an adobe house and it serves as the ideal background for her interests and collections. Tyler has family roots in the

Southwest, and she owns several pieces collected by her family. She is particularly interested in the Navajo culture, as well as Mexico and Africa—all cultures that respect and value artisans.

Tyler boldly mixes appropriately scaled and detailed pieces from a variety of sources to create her signature look. Mirrors from India and a carved Philippine console table that shows a Spanish Colonial influence add to her richly appointed rooms. She has the discipline to search for precise pieces and to avoid overcrowding her small house.

WOULD SOUTHWESTERN WORK FOR YOU? Consider Southwestern if you enjoy rich earthy color and textures along

with rugged furniture and accessories. Southwestern works especially well for decorators who can add texture to the walls with products such as pretextured paint or decorative paint finishes. Although traditional or cottage houses with trims and moldings don't lend themselves to the Southwestern style, ranch-style and contemporary homes can be warmed with Southwestern colors and furnishings. To learn more about this style of decorating, visit stores and dealers who work with Native American, Southwestern, and Mexican artists and artisans. Personal contact is infinitely more instructive than relying solely on Internet access for research and collecting.

Take comfort if all your furniture and art are not in the Southwestern style. As the region continues to attract new residents, traditional vintage furniture and art from the eastern and midwestern United States and abroad frequently become part of Southwestern-style interiors.

EASY STARTING POINTS. Each room requires one or two key furniture pieces to set the tone and anchor the setting. Search for large vintage tables, trunks, or wardrobes (or well-made reproductions). Select rugs that evoke the Southwestern and Native American spirit; use them on floors or hang them on walls as art. If you start with a collection of pottery or baskets, group the collection for impact and upgrade and expand the collection rather than add disparate objects. To focus attention on a painting or other artwork, base a color scheme for the room on the art. If you prefer a neutral scheme, paint the walls the color of sand rather than white. Shades of sand are harmonious with the textures and colors of Southwestern and Native American art and artifacts.

TYLER'S STARTING POINTS. Tyler works with Native American art and artifacts that she inherited from her parents and grandparents. Key pieces include nine paintings that depict Native American tribal dances, as well as vintage rugs,

blankets, and trunks. She uses a few notably large-scale pieces, such as a Mennonite table crafted in Mexico, a reproduction armoire topped by an old trunk, and an oak buffet, to anchor the rooms.

STYLE MAKERS. Furniture from Mexico—rugged tables, carved or leather chairs, and carved, painted trunks—provides the direction for a decidedly Southwestern decor. Strive to acquire pieces that incorporate leather, cowhide, or nailheads (used to trim upholstered pieces). Native American and Mexican pottery, baskets, rugs, clothing, tribal masks, and artifacts enrich a Southwestern-style interior. Regional art reflects the mellow colors of the Southwest.

TYLER'S STYLE MAKERS. Tyler creates backdrops with dramatic color-wash walls. Except for the blue bedroom walls, she favors earthy, mellow colors. Tyler anchors the rooms with large-scale furniture, mirrors, and collected art, avoiding clutter and overload of small pieces and multiple collections. Her well-crafted, similarly scaled pieces—representing the cultures of Africa, the Philippines, and India—work together harmoniously. To unite pieces from diverse cultures, Tyler pays attention to detail and color.

COLORS AND TEXTURES. Tyler balances the drama of wall color in her living room, *page 60,* with a striking white upholstered sofa and a mixture of wood pieces. The tailored sofa allows the handmade pillow, baskets, light fixture, and Mexican furnishings to make the design statement. Pottery, wicker, carved furniture, blankets, and woven rugs blend textures and color tones.

FINISHING TOUCHES. Tyler adds brilliance to her rooms with polished tin, crystals, and silver. Polished tin candle chandeliers contribute an element of romance, while a variety of mirrors reflect light and visually expand small rooms. Candles and a vintage tea and coffee service enrich the romantic quality of private spaces. Pairing objects, such as carved Mexican chairs, leather stools, and mirrors, imposes order in the space.

color

Color: Getting Started. Color, the key to successful decorating, produces a physical and an emotional presence. Color can visually stretch space, raise or lower ceiling heights, and alter emotional levels. As a decorating tool, color is reasonably priced. By understanding color principles, you'll develop an eye for adventurous color combinations.

The Color Wheel. This circular diagram shows relationships between colors and offers a standard formula for decorating. Colors of the rainbow are organized equidistantly around the wheel so you can readily see and use primary, secondary, tertiary, or monochromatic color schemes. **Primary.** Every color originates from either red, yellow, or blue—the primary colors. Of all colors, primary colors are the strongest in form. They provide rooms with brightness and visual bounce. **Secondary.** Equal amounts of two primary colors are mixed to achieve secondary colors—violet, orange, or green. **Tertiary.** Mixing equal measures of one primary and its closest secondary color produces tertiary colors—blue-green, blue-violet, red-violet, red-orange, yellow-orange, and yellow-green. **Monochromatic.** One-

THE COLOR WHEEL

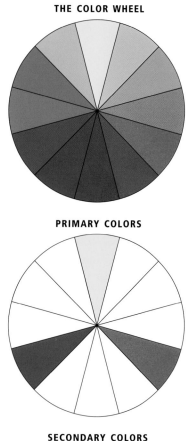

PRIMARY COLORS

SECONDARY COLORS

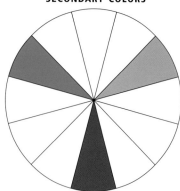

color decorating translates into variations of value and intensity for single colors, or hues. In monochromatic schemes, colors are not competing for attention, so settings are calm (see the room on pages 66–67). **Hue.** Attributes or gradations that classify color as red, yellow, blue (primary); green, orange, violet (secondary); and so on, are referred to as hues. **Value.** The relative lightness or darkness of colors is known as value. For example, sky blue is a light value; cobalt is a dark value. **Intensity.** This term refers to color saturation and specifies clearness or brightness. **Tint.** Closest to white in value, tints are also referred to as pastels. **Shade.** Darkening or dulling colors with black or gray creates shades. **What the pros know.** Paint chip cards typically have light and dark variations of one color, making it easy to choose complementary colors. Use light yellow in one room, for example, and a deeper hue from the same paint chip card in an adjoining room. For delineation, choose colors separated by at least one color chip on a card. To ensure the same intensity for contrasting colors, select hues from the same position on paint chips, using the same paint brand.

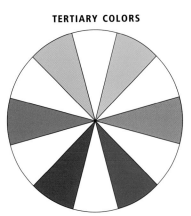

TERTIARY COLORS

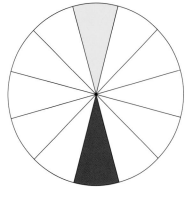

COMPLIMENTARY COLORS

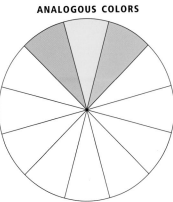

ANALOGOUS COLORS

Assert your personality and decorate with rich hues of your favorite colors balanced by white.

colordefines your world

Pair a beautifully refined shade of red with white and natural hues for a no-fail color palette. Add touches of black and gold in the accessories for a completely sophisticated scheme. Red, the most daring and passionate of colors, infuses this living room with drama and warmth. The primary-plus-white scheme works equally well using deep velvety blue or golden, luminous yellow.

WHY THE LIVING ROOM COLOR SCHEME WORKS

■ With the most square footage, walls make up the most visible space in rooms. Dramatic color can transform a bland wall into the focal point of the room. Designers suggest filling a room with color before all of the furnishings are assembled.

■ Repetition of the focal-point red, here in the toile-style fabric of the ottoman and pillows, unifies the decorating scheme.

■ Liberal use of white woodwork and trim, including the mantel and built-ins, lightens and brightens this intense color-rich room. White also contributes to the fresh, clean look.

■ Natural colors and textures, introduced by the sisal rug and linen upholstery fabric, relax the traditional-style room without competing with the standout red walls.

■ Designers frequently assert that every room needs a touch of black to connote mystery and worldly sophistication, used successfully here. The black urns, displayed on the top shelf of the built-in, are finishing touches. (Classic ways to introduce black are in lampshades and picture frames.)

■ Gold and gilt warm and enrich the room. The picture frame above the mantel and the burnished old-gold mirror frame (page 72) stand out without overpowering the scheme.

RED PLUS GREEN RELAXES TRADITIONAL. Never underestimate the stimulating power of red. Use clear red to rev up a dining room of dark woods and traditional furnishings. To find just the right shade, choose three favorites from paint chips, purchase quart-size cans, and paint poster board or plywood squares with your choices. Look at the painted squares at different times of the day and evening under varying light conditions to choose the red that works best.

HOW RED PLUS GREEN RELAXES.

■ Clashing is a thing of the past. Designers and savvy decorating enthusiasts employ color wheel opposites, such as the red and green in the dining room, *opposite*. The green diamond trim stands out against the white drapery panels without competing with the dominant red. Allowing one contrasting color to dominate results in a harmonious setting.

■ Repetition of key colors and themes, no matter how subtle, unifies a well-decorated room. Red and green repeat in the floral plates and platters as well as on the stylized table linen. The leaf motif of the tablecloth and chandelier and the bamboo-style chair are subtle reminders of natural green colors that cool the dining room.

COBALT BLUE SURPRISES. Keep your options open—and think originally—when you choose the wall color for a family room or great-room. Instead of using safe neutrals or the dominant color from the upholstery, look at ways to magnify an accent color in the backdrop. To get started, work with pattern in an upholstered piece, a rug, artwork, or accessories and pull out one of the minor accent colors. Follow the advice of designers, who recommend choosing a wall color that blends with, rather than matches, another color in the room.

HOW COBALT BLUE SURPRISES

■ In family rooms dominated by a fireplace and furnished with wing chairs, warm earthy colors typically reflect the comfortable setting. The room opposite, however, receives a jolt from glazed deep blue walls. The cool shade sets the stage for refined sophistication and allows the Asian accessories, such as the blue and white ginger jars, to take center stage.

■ Crisp white reflects light, preventing the cool blue wall color from seeming icy cold, *below*. The subtle white repeated on the taupe upholstery is a unifying element.

PERIWINKLE PLAYS. In traditional settings, choose colors and patterns that add a fun and youthful flair. Include generous doses of white and lots of light and mirrors for a pretty yet playful decorating edge. Pair paint and paint finishes with linens to change your rooms whenever the mood strikes—or when you discover a new appealing color.

HOW PERIWINKLE PLAYS

■ Classic furnishings such as the French-style iron bed and bed hanging, *opposite,* never go out of style. Periwinkle and white freshen the look of these timeless pieces. The pillows dress the bed in a toile, a diamond pattern, and a fanciful urn motif. The lightly distressed white cabinet finish and the white sconce contribute contemporary accents to the sophisticated setting.

■ Color takes on dimension when applied as a specialty decorative finish, as in the linen-look bath, *above left.* The delicate color is dragged horizontally and vertically to simulate summery linen fabric. White fabrics further emphasize summer freshness. The flirty chair slipcover is sheer organdy; heavy cotton, banded with nautical periwinkle stripes, covers the vanity. Covered buttons add a tailored finish.

■ The contrast of the diamond wallpaper pattern and the upholstery stripe, *left,* illustrates the power of pattern in a two-color scheme. The extreme verticality of the chair, flanked by display above, plays off the wide horizontal stripes to add a whimsical note to the setting.

GREEN REFRESHES FORMALITY. Lighten up a living room or dining room with a pale tint of classic color. If you've used dark colors such as forest green or deep blue in the past, look at lighter, natural tints to update your furnishings. Consider replacing ornate wallpaper, heavy window treatments, and an abundance of accessories with quiet colors, simple drapery panels, and a few favorite treasures. Use serene colors—such as apple green, stone, or straw—to introduce a current, relaxed decorating direction. If you like decorative paint finishes, choose a simple tone-on-tone color wash to sponge, rag, or blend colors.

HOW APPLE GREEN REFRESHES

■ Classic, timeless pieces, such as the camelback sofa and leather armchairs, set the tone for the living room, *above*. The decorating challenge: Give a fresh look to these investment pieces. The solution: A needlepoint rug, which also

provided the inspiration for the apple green hue on the walls. Although shades of taupe could have been pulled from the rug, the green assigns a wisp of subtle color and coolness to the room. Green also provides a natural background for the landscape painting and other artwork. White woodwork trim and white upholstery support the crisp, tailored look. Minimal pattern allows the apple green to act as a foil for the furnishings without a host of competing colors. Touches of black in the lampshade and rug and the gold in the picture frames enliven the room without altering the relaxed mood.

■ In a room anchored by dark furnishings, such as the leather armchairs and tole table, *above,* the hint of green provides the room with balance. The clear, youthful color also relaxes the formal pieces in the room, such as the marble-top pier table and demilune table. Gilt frames and silver candlesticks stand out against the color as well. As a final touch, the decoratively framed mirrors reflect the polished scene.

YELLOW AND WHITE CHEER. Call on yellow, the happiest and brightest of colors, to infuse a room with sunshine. Crisp white is the perfect foil for this upbeat, winter-taming hue. For a lively look that works with traditional and country decors, choose clear sunny yellow and warm white.

HOW YELLOW AND WHITE CHEER

■ In a pretty Swedish-style bedroom, *right,* white provides the clean canvas for the playful striped window treatments and yellow picture mats. A chair painted white echoes the theme and creates a background for the equally upbeat yellow and white check fabric.

■ Light yellow walls brighten and open the dining room, *left*. Infinitely popular in climates with long winters, yellow is a classic that remains as stylishly appealing by natural daylight as by candlelight or electric light. Oversize check drapery fabric dresses the windows in relaxed yet polished style. For added interest, a stripe fabric with scalloped edges details the cushions of the contemporary-style chairs. Prominent against the cheerful hue are the tole tray and accessories.

■ Shades of white and natural light, *above*, create the perfect foil for yellow as well as for other pretty colors. Yellow appears even brighter and more cheerful when contrasted with white. Carefully edited two-color schemes derive power from color repetition throughout a room. Using a variety of patterns creates interest. Restricting patterns to graphic checks and diamonds in the yellow and white room above, puts a contemporary spin on the country and traditional elements.

BROWN ENRICHES. If modern and contemporary is your decorating bent, consider rich chocolate brown as an alternative to an all-white decor. Brown has the same strong impact as black, but with a warmer, more natural feel. Brown works well with environmental and Asian influences in current contemporary design. Pair with white and naturals for punch and sophisticated power.

WHY BROWN ENRICHES

■ Chocolate brown walls, *left,* make an arresting design statement in a contemporary room that shows an Asian influence. The contemporary white chair looks sculptural against the contrasting color; it has greater impact than it would against white walls. The subtle detailing of art and window treatments add to the look without overshadowing the theme of white and brown.

■ Brown (and other similarly deep colors) can perform successfully in a bedroom, *opposite top,* when the deep hue is paired with and balanced by large doses of white. Beige and warm taupe bridge the contrast and create a quiet appropriate for a bedroom retreat. The upholstered bed further softens the stylish setting, while square and round shapes add interest.

■ Eclecticism rules in this art lover's bedroom office, *opposite bottom.* The energy of the rich chocolate walls plays off the white trim and contemporary lighting, creating a canvas for the rustic painted sawhorse worktable and the ornate chest of drawers. Earthy brown unites diverse furnishings in this harmonious setting. Art pottery and contemporary art and photography in white mats and sleek black frames visually pop against brown walls.

COLOR MODERNIZES CONTEMPORARY. Enjoy sleek contemporary furnishings with colors that allude to the outdoor world. If your contemporary furnishings feature natural wood tones, consider using a soft shade of blue or green for a refreshing backdrop. Employ graphic black and white accents that energize bold forms, sleek lines, and cool modernist designs.

HOW COLOR MODERNIZES.

■ As decorating becomes more personalized, contemporary style embraces colors and patterns from a variety of influences. Interest in the environment, for example, inspires soft natural colors, such as the blue-green in the dining room, *opposite*. The color also recalls the shades of blue, green, and turquoise often used in mid-20th century interiors and furnishings. Such a naturally serene color relaxes the bold lines of the furniture.

■ The richness of natural wood tones, used effectively in modernist houses during the 1960s, warms a 21st-century interior, *above*. The deep wood tones contrast with the natural pale chairs and create a vibrant backdrop for two examples of 20th-century pop art—hung asymmetrically for added visual energy.

GOLD AND JEWELS CREATE DRAMA. Whether your style is traditional or contemporary, incorporate gold and jewel colors to create rooms that have flair and distinction. The key to successfully employing this look is to be bold with these intrinsically regal colors—no halfway measures allowed.

HOW COLOR CREATES DRAMA.

■ Shades and artful touches of gold recall the best of French style, *top right*. This decor works because gold elements are repeated, from the drapery panels and hardware to the chair frame and detailing on the chest. Gilt frames complete the look, while a simple blue and white pillow relaxes the scene.

■ One rich color—here, aubergine (eggplant)—does wonders for a small space, *bottom right*. Chosen to create instant impact and drama, the color acts as a rich contrasting canvas for an art pottery collection displayed on glass shelves. Melon, peach, and orange tones—opposites to purple on the color wheel—enhance the aubergine. Light artwork stands out just as well against the dark color.

■ Gold sparkles and enlivens a comfortably eclectic room of rich browns, *opposite*. Against deep brown walls, the leather sofa creates a quiet and relaxed mood. In contrast, the sunburst mirror—a classic design from the 1950s—and the stylized accent table brighten and refine the space. Adding energy and unifying the color scheme, the hinged four-panel color-block screen features shades of brown and gold as well as metallic hues. Accent pillows provide subtle sheen and stylized pattern.

WHITE IS CONTEMPORARY. A tint of white is an unparalleled canvas for the arresting sculptural shapes of contemporary furniture—and the playful forms and lively colors of modern furnishings and art. White ranges from warm to cool on the color spectrum; it is not a single tint. Look for the palest tint (white with the faintest glimmer of color) that works with your setting, exposure to the sun, and furnishings.

WHY WHITE ROOMS WORK.

■ With furniture as interesting and as artful as this natural wood bed, *right,* no background color is needed. The plain walls and floor allow the shapely natural wood to star. The lively striped light fixture and the chrome floor lamp contribute equally in supporting roles.

■ Clean and cool, the pristine white walls of this living room, *above,* are the backdrop for a pair of armless brown love seats. A pair of painted tables effectively repeats the bright white theme. Pale artwork and ethereal window treatments focus the attention on the hearthside grouping. Minimal accessories reflect the serenity of the space.

■ White walls open the minimally furnished dining room to the French doors and beyond, *opposite bottom.* White plus naturals meld sleek contemporary with relaxed garden-style decorating.

■ Visually quiet and serene, the guest room, *left,* demonstrates the perfection of an all-white room. The play of shapes—rectangular, square, and round—and the tufting and chrome accents complete the decoration without disturbing the sense of peace.

pattern

Patterns and fabrics impart style and personality to your environment. For the most pleasing and professional results, think of them as twin decorating tools. When you plan a room scheme, consider how and where to use pattern—in wallpaper, decorative finishes, carpet, area rugs, upholstery, or draperies. **For the most confident start,** professional designers recommend building schemes **that are based on a dominant pattern.** Large patterned rugs, such as Oriental rugs or abstract contemporary designs, provide a starting point for making other fabric selections. It is much easier to find fabrics to complement rugs than to conduct the search vice versa. **Colors, wall finishes, and fabric patterns** play off the colors and pattern of a rug. When a rug doesn't anchor the decorating scheme, however, designers often suggest giving paint  finishes or dominant fabrics or wallpapers the leading role. **The abundant resources** for applying paint finishes—from books and videos to supplies and specially formulated paints and glazes—make it easy and affordable to use this decorating approach. **The profusion of fabric patterns and wallpapers** in a wide price range is further incentive to find patterns in colorways that work for your style. Colorway refers to a color scheme—three or more color combinations—of fabric and wallpaper patterns and designs. **Ponder pattern and fabric combinations:** The more of both you use in a room, **the livelier the room will be.** To create order in such energetic settings, decorators choose a dominant pattern in the largest scale and work from there. If you like novelty prints—

fabrics or wallpapers that feature recognizable objects such as urns or porcelains—they are a reliable starting point. **The dominant fabric** isn't always used in the greatest quantity: It may be used for wallpaper only, or it may be repeated in wallpaper and matching fabric. You may prefer a neutral pattern for a large-scale application such as a sofa and reserve the dominant pattern for a chair or ottoman. Unless they are used as accents, **supporting patterns** repeat at least one of the colors in the dominant pattern. **Large rooms readily lend themselves to pattern and fabric,** but small rooms can accommodate a lively mix too. For design harmony, cover a pair of matching chairs with matching fabric. **For added decorative interest,** employ different colors of the same pattern to cover matching chairs. To help you in your decorating search, **organize a collection of fabric swatches** and staple them into a binder that you can carry with you as you shop. Note where each fabric could work in your home.

pattern energizes rooms

Take advantage of the decorating potential of pattern when you refresh a furnished room or update vintage furniture. For a sure solution, create a two-color primary palette and then introduce a pattern or two into the mix. Vary the pattern scale as well as the fabric and wallpaper openness (background) for interest. As an alternative to upholstery, use custom-made slipcovers, which allow seasonal transformation or a permanent change.

HOW MULTIPLE PATTERNS WORK.

■ Blue and white, one of the most beloved decorating schemes, cools the bedroom, *opposite,* filled with multiple patterns and fabrics. The print fabric of the sofa slipcover sets the scheme. Color schemes like this one—a hue plus white—allow a mix of patterns to participate without overpowering.

■ Wallpaper enhances without dominating the scheme. The subtle pattern echoes the old-fashioned furnishings, including the vintage painted iron bed. The sheer windowpane check of the draperies, banded in blue, supports the palette. The lampshade has a unifying blue accent.

■ The floral slipcover on the club chair introduces green and pink into the room. These accent colors relax as well as personalize the two-color scheme.

■ Finishing touches pull the room together and create a professional and polished appeal. The low table and floor lamp are painted white, while the cotton rug and quilt are crisp blue and white. Fabrics featuring latticework and a nautical theme deck the sofa pillows. Baskets contribute natural color and texture to the inviting bedroom retreat.

FRESH TAKE ON TOILE. Encourage toile, the classic French scenic print, to take a lighter contemporary direction by pairing the pattern with large doses of white. Relax the setting with a natural-fiber rug and use only minimal favorite accessories. If blue isn't your color choice, toile patterns are printed in well-known color combinations such as black and white, red and white, and green and white. Also consider reverse toiles—the stylized or scenic pattern is white; the background is a color or black.

HOW TO UPDATE WITH TOILE.

■ Tailored white slipcovers and a sisal rug, *above,* contrast with the traditional toile. Although some designers advocate matching toile walls and fabrics, the white slipcovers provide a clean, contemporary balance to the updated sitting room.

■ A touch of toile stands apart, *above right,* as the tie-on slipcover for a reproduction French-style chair. Light and dark woods are both handsome against a toile background.

■ More neutral than a busy print, toile wallpaper frames a traditional harbor print and sailing ship, *right.* The colors and patterns work harmoniously in such traditional areas, although small abstract paintings also make interesting contrast.

■ A few large and closely related accessories, such as the print that leans on the mantel, *opposite,* create more impact against toile than multiple small accessories do.

STRIPES, CHECKS, AND FLORALS. If you love pattern and color, indulge your passion with an upbeat mix of your favorites. Instead of settling for timid interpretations of patterns and pale colors, pair lush, saturated shades with equally vibrant patterns. Use white to balance the backdrop and the fabric backgrounds to restrain a cheerful mix from becoming too energetic.

HOW TO CREATE A BOLD PATTERN MIX.

■ Yellow and white candy cane stripes and oversize checks, *below,* declare assurance that this is a dining room of good cheer. The floral pattern serves as botanical art; the kilim rug anchors the scheme.

■ The engaging living room illustrates how repeating pattern and color relaxes and updates traditional furnishings while linking open living and dining room spaces. The large scale floral pattern boldly balances windows in both areas, but with stylishly different treatments. A larger scale stylized floral with a white background covers the sofa in the foreground. Two similarly scaled stripes contrast and energize. Yellow walls echo the swagged window treatment; yellow repeats in the chair seat and in the floral sofa. Armless chairs add a tailored stripe and subtle plaid. With every upholstered piece contributing pattern, the grouping achieves lively interest.

PATTERN PLUS COLOR.

If you love rich colors and detailed patterns, team up the duo to decorate your cozy spaces. Look for prints or tapestry fabrics with appealing designs, motifs, and color combinations. Begin with a patterned rug or the most dominant fabric and choose supporting prints and solids in the same colors.

HOW TO CHOOSE COLOR PLUS PATTERN.

■ The woven kilim rug, *opposite,* inspires the earthy red and yellow scheme for this sitting area. The toile wallpaper and fabric repeat the mellow colors. Two repeating scenic prints also replicate the vibrant color combination—reversing the background from red to buttery yellow.

■ Designers get the most impact from toile patterns by repeating the lovely print in wallpaper and fabric, *above.* This window treatment features a lush solid red, lined with toile. Tassels stylishly trim the neatly tailored drapery. The solid red of the window treatment repeats in the ruffled fabric lampshade. With pattern as background, uncomplicated, medium tone pieces furnish the room without jarring the setting. As an alternative, the desk or chair could be painted or dressed in yellow or red.

SUBTLE SOPHISTICATION. In rooms where texture reigns, regard pattern in fabric, rugs, and wall treatments as an additional element of the sensual scheme. Combine subdued pattern-on-pattern fabrics with a mix of surfaces and earthy colors.

HOW SUBTLE PATTERNS CREATE MEMORABLE ROOMS.

■ The living room, *opposite,* showcases diverse tastes and collected artifacts from around the world. In this sophisticated setting, traditional pattern-on-pattern damask imparts refinement and balance. The pattern also visually softens the sofa and club chair to prevent them from dominating the room. Diagonally cut striped fabric in the accent pillows enlivens the tailored, monochromatic scheme.

■ A stenciled border over color-washed walls, *below,* interprets pattern with restraint. In this lush setting designed for nighttime dining, a handsome tapestry fabric contributes rusty reds with touches of purple. The matching armless chairs, skirted to the floor, denote grace and comfort and yield a feeling of serenity. Black shades, rather than matching fabric, cap the chandelier candle: a lesson in restraint and neutrality when decorating with patterns.

START WITH A COLLECTION. If you collect and your treasures feature patterned motifs, you may have an engaging starting point for a decorating scheme. Start with your favorite objects and work in congenial fabrics and fresh colors that showcase with style. For the most effective display, concentrate on one type or style—vases or pottery, for example. If your collecting is in a contemporary vein, look for sleek glass, metal, or art pottery pieces.

HOW TO WORK WITH COLLECTIONS.

■ The ultimate patterned collectible, English chintzware pottery and porcelains, *right,* replicate highly detailed printed floral fabric. Collectors mass chintzware, varying the scale and the flowers.

■ Manufactured and exported from the 1920s through the 1950s, painted chintz designs, *below,* transformed everyday objects, such as cups and saucers, into works of art.

■ Chintzware determines the soft, feminine direction and the fresh colors of the living room, *opposite.* Neutral walls and sofa allow the densely painted porcelains to star. Colors in the floral and woven plaid fabrics repeat the hues of the chintzware, while the wing chair visually balances the wall arrangement. The open background of the floral fabric provides pleasing contrast to the tight chintzware designs. Tailored plaid fabric contributes the balance and visual relief that floral decor often needs. Chintzware plates flank the framed art in pairs; teapots and vases are safely stored on the built-in above the cased opening. Wallpaper in the adjoining hallway carries the floral theme in a lighthearted pattern.

REFINING CLASSIC PATTERNS. If you are drawn to colonial styles in furniture and collections, you may already know that vivid pattern and vibrant colors warmed the fine homes of the original 13 American colonies. As you plan a decorating scheme, you'll see traditional fabrics such as pattern-on-pattern damask, woven tapestries, and silks in deep, rich shades. Use these fabrics in a mix of patterns and colors to enliven classic camelback sofas, wing chairs, and ottomans. Repeat colors and patterns as accents to unify this refined look.

HOW TO FRESHEN COLONIAL STYLE.

■ Blue and white Chinese export porcelains, *opposite and above,* prized as much today as they were in the late 18th and early 19th centuries, set the decorating scheme for a living room based on elegant Early American pieces. The patterned Chinese rug reiterates the blue and white scheme and is strengthened by the blue damask covering the camelback sofa. The window treatment adds a related pattern, a crewel-like print that recalls fabrics of the colonial era. The stylized floral pattern on the open-arm chair breaks up the blocks of color in the sofa and wing chair. The faux leopard print pillow imparts a note of playfulness to the historically based look.

■ The faux-grained corner cupboard, a rare New England piece, contributes stylized motifs to the scheme, anchored by the collection of blue and white export china. The swag wallpaper border and the collection of stacked boxes illustrate pattern use in the colonial era.

NOVELTY PRINTS AND PATTERNS. Use novelty patterns—detailed print replicas of easily recognizable objects, figures, or animals—for whimsy and of-the-moment style. Look for prints of porcelains, pottery, urns, garden motifs, and pets in wallpaper and fabrics. You'll often find different colorways of the same pattern printed both as wallpaper and fabric. Translated, that means that the background and major hues are different but the design is the same. Consider novelty prints for classic applications in dining rooms or breakfast areas—or for fun and playful nurseries and older children's rooms.

HOW PATTERNS SET THE SCHEME.

■ Using novelty print wallpaper along with the blue and white Chinese porcelains, *above,* doubles the decorating impact. The scale of the actual plates and the scale of the wallpaper pattern are so close that the two displays meld into one artful wall arrangement.

■ The dining room, *opposite,* features two distinctive patterns. The frond motif lends a hand-painted effect above the wainscoting, while the detailed drapery fabric incorporates a ribbon design. Wallpaper sample books often include fabrics that are designed to complement the featured papers. Both fabric and wallpaper are usually available in several colorways.

COOL DOWN A PLAYFUL MIX. If you want to mix playful patterns in a bedroom while keeping the mood restful and calm, work with soft, grayed-down colors and muted fabrics. To avoid jarring contrasts, look for colors with the same intensity and choose small scale patterns and quiet motifs.

HOW TO CHOOSE RESTFUL PATTERNS.

■ A calligraphy print fabric in celadon green, *opposite,* is the playful, youthful starting point for a room for two young sisters. The fabric repetition—from the draperies to skirted table to pillow shams—strengthens the visual impact of the subtle pattern. The clear blue stripes on the accent pillows and the patterned blue bed skirt reinforce the summery mood created with white coverlets. Contrasting fabrics neatly finish the oversize square shams and the small accent pillows.

■ In the adjacent sitting room, *above,* pattern reigns with a light and capricious hand. Here, the grayed-blue and shades of pink resonate in a mix of patterns and trims. The blue geometric pattern updates a rattan settee, a family piece passed along to the girls. The same pattern gives style and personality to the wing chair, fashionably finished with a ruffled skirt. A patterned pink skirt and an overskirt with tasseled braid disguise a table made of composition board. Checks cover the oversize floor pillow and the neck roll in the wing chair; pink prints add further interest as rectangular accent pillows. The base of the painted table features stylized lambs. The lively and lighthearted mix is restrained with soft colors that create a sense of repose and a retreat for reading, homework, and general relaxing.

Factor art and its presentation into the pattern mix for one-of-a-kind rooms.

decorating quick tips

UPDATE WITH MATS AND FRAMES. Think like an interior designer, and move art and framing from finishing touches to key players in your pattern and color mix. Whether you use original art, prints, posters, or family photographs, consider how the colors and images contribute to the overall scheme. Choose frames and mats that enhance the piece and that work with your total decorating mood as well as other colors and patterns in the room. Although a 3-inch-wide mat is often used for prints, experiment with wider mats for more dramatic effects.

■ **LITHOGRAPHS.** Limited edition color prints, *right,* prized for delicate colors, were discovered at a tag sale. The lithographs illustrate the impact that matting and framing can make on design. The suede-finish moss green mat pairs with a decorative frame for a traditional look that would work well in an English cottage or a formal country-style room. A burled wood frame gives the other print a sleek look that would fit in eclectic decor.

■ **WOODCUTS.** Japanese woodcuts, *opposite, near right,* can wear a variety of frame styles—from faux bamboo to dramatic black. The double matting allows the introduction of a second color for interest. In the bottom example, the repetition of black in the frame and mat visually strengthens the artwork.

■ **PHOTOGRAPHS.** Proper framing and acid-free mats elevate black and white family snapshots, *opposite, far right,* to art. Black and white photographs, which don't fade to the extent of color snapshots, impart a timeless look to a tabletop or wall grouping. A wide mat and chrome frame animate a small snapshot; a frame with corner rosettes dresses up a family vacation snapshot.

LITHOGRAPHS

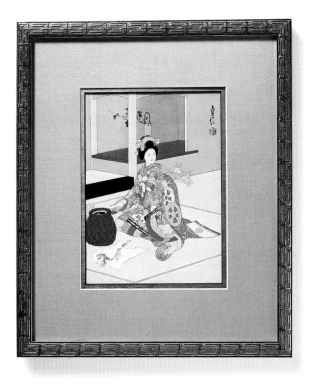

WOODCUTS

PHOTOGRAPHS

window&wall

Window treatments are slimming down and lightening up as 21st-century design moves away from opulence toward edited interiors. If you favor this approach, emulate leading interior designers: In place of heavy top treatments and yards of side panels, substitute understated drapery panels hung on exposed rods.

Where a rich or lush appearance is desired, let fabric rather than fabrication be the star. This is an affordable option because the current fashion trend often requires less fabric than the lavish styles of the past two decades. When beautiful fabric dominates the scene, layers of dressmaker details and trims are superfluous. Although puddling—several inches of fabric that pools luxuriously on the floor—is still popular, consider tailored draperies that neatly graze or hover above the floor. In line with decorating lightly, rediscover the versatility of crisp overscale checks and tone-on-tone woven fabrics. Such stylish fabrics work to abbreviate traditional styles—including Country French and American country—as well as rooms decorated with contemporary flair. Beyond the tailored applications, the return to romance in decorating spurs interest in sheer fabrics, which are sometimes embroidered or appliquéd. When privacy is required, pair sheers with blinds or shades. In

addition to white and off-white fabrics, sheers are available in soft hues, such as pale blues and greens, and metallic sheers lend a sophisticated tone to handsomely decorated living and dining rooms. For texture, choose burlap or similar woven natural fabrics for either casual or formal settings. With the trend

toward less complicated treatments, you'll see a variety of applications for classic Roman shades. Fabric and trims determine the degree of formality for Roman shades. When windows aren't the focal point, neutral fabrics, such as unbleached cotton duck, work well for this tailored application. Roman shades are ideal for windows of varying widths and for rooms with combinations of windows and French doors. For versatility and ease of installation, classic cafe curtains have timeless style. Cafe curtains work equally well alone or combined with modest valances or side panels. For quick solutions to window decorating, purchase ready-made versions of cafe curtains, drapery panels, or Roman shades. Choose hardware that flatters the fabrics and helps guide the decorating direction. Purchase rods and hardware from home furnishing stores or decorating catalogs and hang your window treatments in style.

windowsframe your view

Use window treatments to polish and refine rooms, much as professional designers do. Even when window treatments aren't needed for privacy or sun control, beautiful fabric gathered on handsome rods has a softening effect. Choose fabric colors to blend rather than to contrast with your walls; minimize trim and embellishments for a current yet classic style. If you use ready-made drapery panels, select a woven pattern-on-pattern or subtle stripe fabric that blends with the wall color. For a similar effect, a colored sheer can be used.

WHY THESE WINDOW TREATMENTS WORK.

▨ Burlap panels warm a sitting room filled with a mix of classic and contemporary furnishings. The generous use of drapery panels balances the strong lines of these furniture styles, and the contrasting band adds a neat finish. The woven fabric provides weight and texture without appearing unduly heavy. To admit maximum light, drapery panels hang from a rod that curves outward and extends beyond the French doors. This solution also prevents fabric from interfering with traffic through the doorway. At dusk, the treatments create a sense of enclosure and privacy.

▨ The natural burlap blends with burlap walls which have been striped with silver felt-tip pens to enhance the neutral, monochromatic scheme of warm taupe, cream, and white. Operable pinch-pleat burlap panels, attached inside the window casing, pair with shades at side windows where privacy is needed. Natural wood blinds or natural cotton Roman shades would create a similar tailored effect.

TREATMENTS BLOCK LIGHT. Give your television room or den the feel of a media center with light-blocking and light-controlling window treatments. If you have a large screen television and watch sports or movies during the day, use shades and blinds to create a movie theater effect. If you order window treatments or have them custom made, ask about ordering blackout lining, which is typically used for bedroom windows. The lining can be incorporated in a variety of window treatments—from draperies and curtains to bamboo shades. As an alternative, use old-fashioned roller shades, which are sold in a variety of colors and weights, or purchase a fusible shade kit from a fabric store to cover a shade in your own fabric.

HOW WINDOW TREATMENTS BLOCK LIGHT

■ The covered cornice, *above,* repeats the natural woven fabric used for the wall panels. Wood blinds control light without making a loud design statement. The natural wood balances the room's brilliant purple walls and high-tech surfaces and furnishings.

■ Fabric window panels with blackout lining lower to transform the family room into a screening room. To create a gallery effect, the window panels are in the same design and fabric as wall panels that frame art. The natural color dramatically stands out against the deep purple walls and is repeated in the room's eclectic mix of furnishings.

ARTFUL HANGING. Consider hardware as jewelry that adds just the right finishing touch to drapery panels. Choose hardware, including finials, to complement the style, fabrication, fabrics, and other trims. Shop at fabric stores, home centers, and discount stores for interesting hardware, rings, finials, and other window treatment accessories.

HOW TO HANG ARTFULLY.

■ In a room of pale and natural tones, dark metal drapery hardware echoes the dark furnishings, *above*. The metal tones contrast with the soft yellow, making the hardware become an accessory in its own right. For the most graceful effect, the drapery hangs from midway between the top of the window frame and the ceiling. Hanging drapery panels above the window casings adds height to the small space and balances large furniture pieces, such as the rust red Asian chest. Metal accents are repeated in the chest ornamentation, a small accent table, and a wire basket. The classic overscale check and the pinch-pleated drapery panels add polish to the room.

Beautiful rooms deserve stunning window treatments, *above*. In design simplicity, this translates into lined silk drapery panels gently roped to a gilded drapery rod. Brackets and shell-motif finials are restrained finishing touches. Tailored Roman shades in matching fabric present a practical and stylish solution for the French doors.

Sheer fabrics delicately diffuse light and soften unadorned windows in the dining room, *left*. For instant drama and to heighten the effect of the patterned sheer, brackets support the drapery rod just below the molding. Delicate stylized finials and even more delicate drapery rings recall handcrafted gold jewelry.

UPDATED ROMAN SHADES. When you need practical and versatile window treatments, recall Roman shades. These classic window treatments solve a variety of problems—excessive sunshine, lack of privacy, and unmatched windows, for example. In lively prints with added trim, they work magic in fresh 21st-century style. Because of the simplicity of construction, custom-made Roman shades are usually affordable; patterns are also available to help you sew your own. Handsew or hot-glue embellishments to update ready-made Roman shades.

HOW TO UPDATE ROMAN SHADES.

■ In the comfortable sitting room, *right,* botanical print fabric converts Roman shades into a work of art. Solid fabrics are commonly associated with Roman shades, but detailed prints introduce a lively, fresh look. Tasseled trim adds extra detailing usually seen only on formal treatments.

■ Roman shade construction allows the fabric to hang flat. Instead of being pulled tightly to the top of the window casing, the fabric displays itself to full advantage, *below.*

FANCY AND FRUGAL. Look for creative ways to stretch your window treatments budget. To save money on fabrics and trims, shop at fabric outlets, including internet sources. (See page 160) When you use floor-length treatments, don't skimp on the fullness of the style. Instead, shop for budget-priced fabrics, such as blends that imitate the texture and sheen of silk. If privacy and sun control aren't issues, select fixed drapery panels, fixed shades, or simple valances to save on fabric. For privacy along with fabric conservation, choose tailored cafe curtains or Roman shades.

HOW TO BALANCE STYLE AND BUDGET.

■ Galvanized steel pipes, *opposite,* take a stylish turn as drapery rods for French doors. Finials and drapery rings made of unfinished wood are decoratively painted to match the steel. To open the room to daylight and views, the rod extends beyond the French doors. Lined panels reduce fabric damage from the sun.

■ The 6-inch bouillon-style trim that details the draperies is repeated on the pleated table skirt, *below,* adding a splurge of luxury to the room.

SHEER METALLICS. Pair sheer and shine for fashionable window treatments that refresh traditional interiors and relax contemporary settings. Shop for gossamer fabrics that have a metallic glow and a hint or stronger tint of color; choose a hue that reflects the direction of your color palette—from either the warm or cool side. Fabricate the shimmering textile into plain panels, gently gathered treatments, soft curtains, or swags.

HOW TO USE METALLIC FABRICS.

■ In a living room of family treasures, *right and opposite,* the amber tint of the gossamer fabric diffuses light and balances the dark wood furnishings. A coppery glow radiates into the setting, working well with the rich woven fabrics as well as the dark wood. The fabric's pattern-on-pattern weave subtly echoes the texture of the tapestry armchair and the Oriental rug. Slight drapery puddling gently grazes the floor.

■ For detailing and dramatic effect, the drapery rod and finials, *left,* are decoratively glazed to look like copper. Gathering the fabric into artful rosettes and graceful swags creates a youthful yet polished and luxurious look. The rosettes are held to the drapery rings by stitching through the fabric.

■ Sophisticated window treatments fabricated from Italian gossamer fabric animate a living room full of comfortably overstuffed furniture and vintage pieces, *opposite.* For the most lavish and noticeable effect, rods are attached just below the crown molding to allow the panels to float along the height of the living room walls. The dark walls, a saturated grayed blue-green, balance the richness of the Oriental rug, while the translucent window treatment lightens with shimmer and shine. The contrasting wall color also allows the glistening fabric to become a distinctive counterpoint among the dark furnishings.

INEXPENSIVE ELEGANCE. Combine stylish designs with budget priced quality fabrics to create a style that enhances your decorating scheme and saves you time and money. To avoid waste and get the most for your money, measure windows accurately before ordering. Measure the drop (length) for draperies from the point where you intend to install the rod to the place where you want the draperies to fall. For width, measure the full length of the rod; double or triple the width measurement for the desired fullness. If you use narrow ready-made panels, seam two panels together to avoid a skimpy look.

HOW TO CUT FABRIC COSTS.

Unlined tabbed drapery panels, *opposite,* diffuse light and soften tall French doors in the comfortably furnished great-room. Tabs provide the necessary support for heavy fabric to hang gracefully from the decorative metal rods. Budget-stretching unlined panels require minimal sewing, have a less structured look, and screen light without completely blocking the view. Add cotton lining or shades for more privacy or sun control.

Natural unbleached cotton fabric, *above left,* becomes an enhancing background for vintage pieces and fabrics that shine. The economical, softly gathered fabric is ideal for full drapery panels and curtains. Shades, wood blinds, or sheers pair well with the panels for added privacy or for sun and temperature control. Cream or off-white ready-made sheers blend with the natural cotton; crisp white sheers create contrast.

Natural unlined burlap becomes stylishly sophisticated when made into sleek Roman shades, *above right.* For the neat look and clean lines, the shade attaches to a concealed cornice board and gently wraps the window. Natural raffia fringe adds the finishing touch. Burlap lined with a soft natural cotton would yield a more structured, tailored look. Such treatments pair well with a bifold shutter in natural or painted wood, wood blinds, or an insulated cellular shade for privacy. Lined natural cotton duck also works well for Roman shades when privacy and temperature control are desired.

SWAGGED FOR FUN. In a room where you want your eye to move up rather than out, consider the possibilities of graceful swag treatments. Depending on the fabric and degree of detail, use the swag alone or pair it with rosettes, jabots to the side, or drapery panels. Employ swags as glamorous treatments that also conceal the tops of less-than-perfect windows or frames, or use deep swags to visually raise low or out-of-scale windows for more pleasing proportions. Consider a full-fledged swag and jabot treatment for a room where you want a dressy look, such as the dining room. For a relaxed look, hang a gathered swag. As an alternative to drapery panels, update the swag with softly tinted sheers or a shutter. To create a contemporary look, choose a fabric that matches or blends with the wall color and hang the swag without rosettes or other ornamentation.

HOW TO USE SWAGS.

■ The fanciful swag for a child's playroom, *below,* is a decoratively painted plywood cornice board that is attached with wood screws and angle brackets. This decorative painting technique, trompe l'oeil, means "fool the eye" in French. The artful, clever cornice is hand-painted by a decorative artist, but commercial stencil motifs could be used instead.

■ A traditional swag, fabricated from a sophisticated floral and complementary check, finishes the handsomely furnished dining room, *opposite.* The fabric mix and the asymmetrical arrangement relax the formality of the treatment. This fixed treatment requires less fabric than treatments with operable panels do.

STYLISH EXTRAS. Create one-of-a-kind window treatments by mixing fabrics and fabrications and adding drapery rods and hardware that contribute to the design.

HOW TO ADD PERSONAL TOUCHES.

▨ Two blending shades of lilac convey contemporary color block flair to standard bedroom drapery panels, *above.*

▨ In a breakfast room, *above right,* striped drapery panels edged with bias-cut fabric frame the view. Cafe curtains diffuse light and provide a degree of privacy, while rods and rings ease opening and closing.

▨ Gently tailored shades, fabricated in a wide cotton seersucker stripe, *right,* answer the question of how to dress two corner windows. The woven fabric and soft lining relax the look, which is less tailored than traditional Roman shades.

▨ Striped valances contribute nautical crispness to the bath, *opposite, top left.* Concealed blinds provide privacy.

▨ Vintage tablecloths, too beautiful to store, create delicate window treatments, *opposite, top right,* a romantic complement to the carved French bed and delicate linens.

▨ Bracketed hardware contributes distinctive style in a bedroom graced with breezy sheers, *opposite, bottom left.*

▨ Sheers, held in place by curtain tiebacks, *opposite, bottom right,* display an easy folded back treatment.

Build a palette and a decorating scheme from your window treatment fabric.

decorating quick tips

START WITH FABRIC. Whether you decorate from scratch or refresh a room, work as designers do to create a mix of patterns, colors, and textures. A pleasant mix is achieved by blending. For example, *below,* the rich color of the floral window treatment fabric initiates the scheme. Colors from the floral repeat in the stripe, check, and quilted fabrics. Wall color may also be based on the floral. See page 160 for fabric source.

■ **WARM COLOR PALETTE.** One floral fabric offers a wide range of choices. For an inviting, comfortable look, a mellow buff tone is pulled from a traditional floral, *above.* The hint of gold places the fabric on the warm side of the color wheel. Warm colors are ideal for rooms with cool exposures and are favored in climates with long, cold winters. Mellow warm colors are also favored for their light reflecting qualities. To work confidently with color, make your own sample boards incorporating fabric and paint chips. To determine how light or dark to take your color choice, find a paint chip card with a color you like and paint a sample board with that color. Next, paint sample boards with the lighter tint and the darker shade of the same color (these appear on either side of your first choice on the paint chip card). Intensity and degree of color increase when color covers large areas. Gold colors, such as the subtle buff in the floral fabric, appear vibrant over a large wall. All colors—particularly neutrals with hints of yellow—change throughout the day in response to changes in natural and artificial light.

■ **COOL COLOR PALETTE.** Cool colors, such as grayed blue, *above,* function well in rooms with sunny, west-facing exposures. Mixing gray with a color lowers the color's intensity. Rooms painted with a color from the cool palette work in the winter as well as in the summer. The winter sun warms the room, and pale hues reflect winter light. A grayed blue, which hints at color without overpowering the room, appears fresh and youthful while creating light, open interiors. The shade works well with light woods and white furniture in current design trends. The darker blue in the fabric could be used for dramatic effect in a nighttime dining room or a powder room, but it might overpower a living area or bedroom. If you don't find the exact shade you want from a paint chip, have a standard chip color lightened or darkened at the paint store and experiment on poster board. When you alter colors, save the paint can and labels so that room colors can be mixed to the specifications you've created. This is also helpful if you plan to retouch or use the color for another room.

■ **NATURAL COLOR PALETTE.** Colors inspired by nature freshen and update traditional, country, and contemporary interiors. Ivy green reflects the lighter tones of leaves in the print fabric, *above.* Similar to shades of blue and gray, greens lighten and open for a serene, soothing effect. For the most natural and pleasing appearance, recall the extensive range of greens found in nature, including pale spring shades and the mellow green-gold shades of autumn. If you attempt to match exact shades of green, you may need to experiment. If a green is too cool, for example, work with shades of green that have a touch of yellow—such as apple green. When green seems too heavy and saturated, adjust the shade to palest mint or celadon, which is based on the well-known Chinese porcelain. Celadon or seafoam may have a blue cast that adds dimension. When you use pale hues of green, you'll see dramatic differences throughout the day and all through the seasons.

furnishings

Think like a professional decorator to create comfortable, well-appointed rooms.
Typically, decorators and decorating enthusiasts start a room by
focusing on one or two furniture pieces. For example, with a sofa or a pair of
love seats as the cornerstone of the design scheme, your room decor and
furniture plan can be based on the pattern, color, scale, and
size of the pieces. Keep in mind that quality-made classic sofa
shapes in solid neutral colors work in a variety of schemes and
transcend fads. With normal use, well-made sofas last a
lifetime or more. Savvy decorators recommend purchasing
quality-built used sofas from thrift stores or consignment
shops rather than purchasing unsubstantial new sofas. It's
possible to locate vintage sofas as well as sturdy reproduction
pieces in traditional and contemporary styles. Although sofas

typically anchor living rooms, love seats often fit small rooms better. When the
major pieces are in place, choose and arrange the supporting pieces. The most
memorable rooms are based on pieces that relate in proportion, scale, and style—
without necessarily matching—illustrated throughout this book. Even
though individually choosing each chair and table takes time, the result is more
personal than the look of matched sets. Rooms and homes also reflect

personality when collections and art are key design elements. Color schemes and fabric choices based on paintings and collections enliven rooms, **creating interest and individuality.** Consider items that are significant to you and your family and that display well. **For living areas,** look for artwork that will anchor

the room. Frame large-scale art or museum-quality posters and maps, or buy affordable original art or pottery at university, college, art school, or community art shows. **Hunt for artwork and pottery at flea markets and antiques shops to re-create the vintage looks** of country, cottage, or garden decorating styles. Collectors look for well-executed paintings by skilled amateurs, called Sunday painters, who painted for their own pleasure. **To make the most of your art,** highlight it with picture lights purchased from home furnishings stores or frame shops. **As you incorporate art and family photographs into your scheme,** carefully plan whether to match, mismatch, or contrast matting and framing. Mats and frames that coordinate with snapshots, sketches, or children's paintings can turn these personal pieces into works of art. **An interesting current trend** is to make small paintings, prints, and photographs even more significant with dramatically wide double mats.

Anchor every room with one starting-point piece
that fits your decorating style and budget.

furnishings add comfort

Consider your definition of comfort; then use your personal
checklist to add and arrange furniture, lighting, art, and
accessories that work for you. Comfortable rooms are achieved
by decorating to create a personal haven—whether you prefer
cozy rooms decorated with vintage pieces, books, and collections;
uncluttered minimalist spaces; or somewhere in between.
Furnishings comprise more than the basic and the distinguished
furniture pieces; they include lamps, artwork, rugs, mirrors, books,
collections, family photographs, and personal mementos that
add character and personality.

THE WELL-FURNISHED ROOM.

■ Two handsome unmatched sofas anchor the seating area near
the fireplace, *right*. The arrangement creates a congenial grouping
with maximum seating—and an immediate sense of welcome into
the room. The customary setting of facing the sofa toward the
hearth and the sofa back toward the room would make traffic
through this room awkward.

■ Classic camelback and American Empire-style sofas are
mainstays of traditional style. Upholstered versions work in formal
interpretations, while pieces re-covered in stripes or nontraditional
fabrics become sculptural elements in contemporary rooms.

■ Console tables behind the sofas hold overflow art books and
provide the proper height for reading lamps. The butler's tray
coffee table is at home in the traditional setting.

■ Individual vintage armchairs assure interest—and are easier
to acquire than matching pairs.

■ Books create a sedate feeling while the mantel mirror reflects
the handsome scene. The candlesticks are part of a collection.

COLLECTIONS INSPIRE. If you have a collection or two that you love, concentrate your treasures in one room. Grouping a collection of large pieces in one room or arranging smaller objects on one tabletop creates more impact than scattering them throughout the house. Be creative and strive for the most interesting effect. For instance, extend beyond standard wall arrangements by displaying large artwork on an easel, or purchase small tabletop easels to display miniatures. For an artful scene, create a vignette that melds a tabletop display with the wall behind.

HOW TO USE A COLLECTION.

■ Collectible painted tole trays, *left,* enhance a sitting room as works of art and period style. Tole is the French term for sheet metal; however, much of the tole collected today was made in 19th-century England and the United States. Hand-painted swags and borders frame the wall-hung trays for visual interest. The frames of the love seat and settee, intricately detailed with painted medallions, repeat the shapes of the stylized trays. The same painted motifs age a 1940s tray-on-stand to fit with the classical scene.

■ The juxtaposition of the rectangular and round tray, *top right,* relaxes the symmetrical arrangement and introduces an amiable note in a room furnished with rather formal pieces. Charcoal gray upholstery fabric reflects the drama of the black trays, while the painted-frame tray table echoes the vertical wall border, painted swags, and the painted trim on the sofa. The repetition creates a strong visual statement that centers attention on the trays.

■ Trays, trays, everywhere, illustrate the effect of varied heights for a grouped collection, *bottom right.* From an easel display to the balance that is achieved from trays that hang on both sides of the window, the trays receive special attention. The tray displayed on the writing table shares space with art supplies and a reading lamp; the trays propped against the wall provide visual movement within the room.

FURNITURE AS ART. Choose each piece of furniture and each accessory carefully to avoid disappointing design mistakes. Although it takes patience to acquire well-crafted (though not necessarily expensive) furnishings, the result of careful purchasing will be timeless backbone pieces for your design scheme. Resist the temptation to fill your rooms with small collections or make-do pieces, and resist the impulse for immediate gratification. Many little expenditures can quickly add up to the price of one quality piece of furniture or artwork. Observe the lines and scale of classic and historic furniture, and expect to re-cover upholstered pieces.

HOW TO USE FURNITURE AS ART.

■ Less is more in rooms where each piece is chosen with care and an eye to the long-term. The curvy George III settee, *opposite, top left,* pairs with a tapestry that is chosen for its patina rather than its pedigree.

■ Carefully chosen, edited accessories transcend decoration and become art objects. An English Regency mahogany library stand, *opposite, top center,* holds books and other treasures. The lamp, converted from a candlestick, illuminates a beautifully crafted wood box and a framed antique wallpaper fragment. The vignette aptly illustrates creative decorating liberties using display objects.

■ A spare background and minimal accessories allow beautiful pieces to stand out, *opposite bottom.* The mirror features split glass and is designed to appear antique. Flanking finials, which are architectural salvage, provide visual height and balance the tall mirror. Their distressed finish adds an element of age to bridge the gap between the antique furnishings and contemporary objects such as the glass coffee table.

■ The French walnut-frame sofa, *above,* re-covered in a linen and silk twill, appears all the more sculptural because of its subtle, neutral fabric. The facing sofa provides comfortable seating and soft lines that complement without visually competing with the space. The diamond pattern sisal rug and drapery panels contribute soothing and sophisticated finishing touches.

UPDATE AND UNIFY. Tame the chaos and impose order in a room filled with vintage furniture, multiple elements, and small objects. Re-cover old-fashioned upholstered pieces in contemporary fabrics. Introduce current objects, such as lamps, lampshades, a contemporary painting, or accessories, to avoid a museum or period look. Pair objects

from your collections to create symmetry. Group, rather than scatter, small items—such as framed family photographs—to establish a tabletop art gallery. Collect and display frames of interesting shapes, materials, and sizes. Mix current snapshots and copies of old family photographs with books and small treasures.

HOW TO UPDATE AND UNIFY.

■ The re-covered vintage sofa anchors the living room, *opposite*. Oversize pillows update the shape and design. Candlestick lamps highlight family photographs grouped on a marble-top chest. The faux leopard fabric and a French garden chair introduce playful elements in a room of family furniture and collections.

■ Objects are edited and showcased on the mantel, *top*. The pair of Staffordshire hounds, elevated on collected antique books, flank the pinecone-filled tole cachepot to visually bridge the space between the mantel and the landscape painting.

■ Contemporary Italian silk pendants, *above*, illuminate the vignette of framed photographs and mementos. Collected porcelains displayed on stands surround the candelabra bronze. Feathers, in a pair of vases, recall Victorian collections of natural objects.

ANCHORED BY A FIREPLACE. If your living room includes a fireplace and mantel, you have a focal point for your furniture grouping and art display. Balance the scale of the furniture pieces and accessories to create a comfortable seating arrangement. Consider seasonally rearranging the furniture as well as changing the art on the mantel.

HOW TO ANCHOR WITH A FIREPLACE.

■ The classic arrangement of facing the sofa toward the fireplace works well with two accent chairs and a coffee table, *opposite.* The rug organizes the seating grouping, while the glass-top coffee table shifts the focus to the fireplace and mantel. The symmetry of the urns flanking the centered painting completes the orderly arrangement.

■ Two matching facing sofas, *top right,* provide maximum comfortable seating for a conversation oriented living area. In a smaller living area, two love seats or four chairs would work as well. The successful arrangement permits a view of the sparely dressed mantel from every seat. The large framed bull's-eye mirror and capital E stand out with minimalist style against the unadorned backdrop. A pharmacy-style lamp ensures comfortable illumination for reading.

■ An ornate columned oak mantel in a city apartment, *bottom right,* serves as gallery display for a collection of pottery and framed and matted black and white photography. The cane and Haitian painting are travel mementos. Cotton duck slipcovers and a colorful woven cloth are the furniture's summer dress.

WHEN FURNITURE FLOATS. To arrange open spaces in great-rooms, living rooms, or dining rooms, plan furniture groupings that create conversation zones. For long and narrow rooms, break up the galley impression by angling furniture pieces. Angle a rug to define seating areas, and angle sofas or pairs of chairs within the grouping. An armoire or wardrobe angled against corner walls presents a decorative front that adds to the visual interest of the room.

HOW TO FLOAT FURNITURE IN A ROOM ARRANGEMENT.

■ In a large living room, *above,* upholstered pieces are pulled away from the walls to avoid a vast open floor effect. The sofa, anchored by a console table at the back and accent tables to the sides, balances the grouping while floating in the center of the room. Instead of a conventional coffee table, an antique leather seaman's trunk offers visual weight to the grouping. The secretary, placed against the wall, displays a collection of porcelains and seashells.

■ Multiple conversation areas are essential to making a large room feel comfortable, *above*. Organized by the trunk coffee table, the main sitting area incorporates the sofa, an open-arm chair, and a pair of club chairs and ottoman. A trio of period nesting tables affords surface space for drinks and accessories. This large area subdivides easily into two conversation areas: one with two chairs, and the other with the sofa and the open-arm chair. The love seat at the window is removed from the main scene and adds a more private conversation area during parties. For a calm, summery setting, slipcovers of ivory cotton duck relax and unify the traditional upholstered pieces. Silk and Raffia pillows add texture to the yards of white. The narrow lamp table contributes surface display without obstructing the traffic path. The black lampshade and pair of metal urns give weight to the grid of botanical prints. When furniture is pulled toward the center of a room, walls lend themselves to such gallery-style art arrangements.

ARTFUL DINING. Recognize the display potential in your dining area. Whether your dining room is a designated space or a cozy corner of the living area or kitchen, add favorite art and collections to make it more inviting. As little as one wall or a nook provides space for stylish arrangements.

HOW TO CREATE ARTFUL DINING.

■ The antique dresser, *below,* serves the dual purpose of fashionable display and storage for linens, silver, and serving pieces. Such shelves work well to neatly organize favorite pieces, here a collection of brown and white transferware, a pair of Staffordshire spaniels, and horn-handle knives in a silver loving cup. For maximum display, three transferware plates hang above the dresser. If a server or sideboard does not have open storage, display collected platters or plates on stands. In country settings, standing or wall-mount cupboards are another practical option.

■ When space is tight or when a dining room is used only occasionally, a drop leaf table, *above,* can fulfill dining and display requirements. Such tables, which are easy to find in new, vintage, or antique pieces, take up minimal space when they are collapsed. For drama in this small dining area, one large contemporary still life hangs above the tabletop display. Attractive folding dining chairs, such as bamboo types, to accommodate large groups are available from home furnishings stores and decorating catalogs.

■ Softly lit built-in shelves, *opposite,* call attention to the artful display in this dining room. The mix of baskets, finials, books, and framed family photographs mirrors the equally eclectic pairing of the rustic plank table with sleek Louis XVI-style reproduction dining chairs. White pottery pieces displayed on graduated shelves of a bamboo étagère echo the room's striking white trim. When a built-in isn't an option, a decorative vintage or new baker's rack can provide stylish, well-organized display. Picnic baskets and other baskets are ideal for concealed storage.

MEANS OF DISPLAY. If you collect with a passion, space is always at a premium. To fully appreciate your collectibles, look for ways to incorporate them into everyday decorating.

HOW TO FIND DISPLAY FOR YOUR PASSIONS.

■ A large dresser, *above,* organizes an extensive collection of chintzware porcelains. The display illustrates the decorating power of grouping collections for maximum impact and interest.

■ When space is tight, a collector gets creative, *top right,* using room under the table for an antique birdcage and the wainscoting as a mini gallery for framed prints.

■ Posters and photographs, *right,* are recognized and treated as prized art collections. Framed black and white photographs animate the dining room of this late 19th-century apartment. The scale of the tall ceilings lends itself to large art such as the poster, which contrasts with the traditional chandelier.

■ Meticulously displayed musical instruments of different sizes transform a corner into a mini museum, *opposite, top left.*

■ Three tole trays, *opposite, top right,* are arranged in a striking focal point display.

■ Majolica pottery pieces, *opposite, bottom left,* fill a corner cupboard with the colors and motifs of nature.

■ When collectors run out of tabletops, they look for other venues. Here, majolica plates orbit a mirror, *opposite, bottom right.*

TULIP BASE: HOURGLASS AND BELL SHADES

Find the perfect lampshade to turn a classic base into your design statement.

decorating quick tips

SHADES OF DIFFERENCE. Whether you freshen a dated lamp or purchase a new one, take advantage of the wonderfully creative shapes, materials, colors, and trims of lampshades. For the best results when you change shades, make sure the shade is in proportion and scale to the lamp. The decorative top of the base should be visible; the lightbulb and its housing should not. Lamp shops can change the harp (the attachment for the shade) to adjust the proportion of the shade to the lamp. Add new finials to complete the look. See page 160 for source.

■ **TULIP BASE: HOURGLASS AND BELL SHADES.** Organic shapes, such as the tulip base table lamp, *right,* work well for traditional, eclectic, and contemporary settings. The striped hourglass shade provides a retro look, recalling barrel shapes of the '50s and '60s. The classic bell shade puts a traditional spin on the handsome piece.

■ **CANDLESTICK BASE: PAGODA AND SMALL SQUARE SHADES.** Candlestick bases, *opposite, near right,* fit nicely where pairs of lamps are needed—on sideboards, accent tables against the wall, or mantels. The red pagoda shade adds whimsy to relax a traditional setting, or it can act as a lighthearted accent for a bedroom or breakfast room. The handsome square shape is a timeless classic that works well with Country French, English, and American traditional settings.

■ **URN-ON-STAND BASE: PLEATED AND OCTAGON SHADES.** Available in a variety of materials and price ranges, urn bases, *opposite, far right,* are standard shapes. The material of the base and the decorative detail determine the degree of formality. Originally purchased at a department store sale, this lamp features a plain pleated shade and plain finial. For an alternative look, the shade is replaced with a octagon parchment shade, which is topped with a wood finial. A new harp ensures that the shade hangs correctly.

CANDLESTICK BASE: PAGODA AND SMALL SQUARE SHADES　　　**URN-ON-STAND BASE: PLEATED AND HEXAGON SHADES**

CONTRIBUTORS/RESOURCES

Translating Traditional: Seabrook Wallcoverings 800/238-9152, Benjamin Moore Paints 800/826-2623; Emily Minton, photography
The Art of Color: Hilary Rose; Jon Miller of Hedrich Blessing, photography
Fresh '50s Funk: Matt and Christi Strelecki, Wade Scherrer; King Au/Studio Au, photography
When Collections Are Key: Susan Andrews; Bob Greenspan, photography
Country French Ambience: Susan and Jack Arnold, Nancy Ingram; Gene Johnson/Hawks, photography
Color It Contemporary: Benjamin Clavan Architect, Laura Hull; Tommy Miyasaki, photography
Country Colonial: Stuart L. Disston, AIA; David E. Austin, AIA; Austin Patterson Disston; D.J. Carey; Jeff McNamara, photography
Southwestern Spirit: Tyler Atkinson, Claudia Franklin; Christian Bloc, photography
Color Defines: Elizabeth Sullivan Interior Design (pages 70-71), Cynthia Walters Interiors (pages 72-73), Lynn McBride; Cheryl Dalton, photography
Cobalt Blue: Deborah Hastings; Emily Minton
Green Refreshes Formality: Elizabeth Sullivan Interior Design, Lynn McBride, Cheryl Dalton
Subtle Sophistication: Deborah Hastings, Kelly Amen, Emily Minton Fran Brennan
Cool Down a Playful Mix: Diane Carroll, Jenifer Jordan, photography
Window and Wall opening location: Kelly Amen, Joetta Moulden, Fran Brennan
Sheer Metallics: Kelly Amen, Fran Brennan.
Artful Hanging: Camille Saum, ASID, Interior Design (plaid draperies, dining room sheer); Christina Haire, ASID, (yellow draperies on decorative rod); Linda Krinn, Gordon Beall
Updated Roman Shades: Christina Haire, ASID; Linda Krinn; Gordon Beall, photography
Fancy & Frugal: Joetta Moulden, Fran Brennan
Sheer Metallic: Kelly Amen, Fran Brennan
Start With Fabric: Calico Corners, www.calico-corners.com
Furniture as Art: Sue Burgess, Heather Lobdell, Gordon Beall
Update and Unify: Cynthia Walter Interiors, Lynn McBride, Cheryl Dalton
Decorating Quick Tips: Wade Scherrer, Pete Krumhardt, photography
Lamps: (pages 158-159, except far right), Jamie Young Company, 888/671-5883, www.jamieyoung.com

U.S. UNITS TO METRIC EQUIVALENTS

To Convert From	Multiply By	To Get
Inches	25.4	Millimeters (mm)
Inches	2.54	Centimeters (cm)
Feet	30.48	Centimeters (cm)
Feet	0.3048	Meters (m)

METRIC UNITS TO U.S. EQUIVALENTS

To Convert From	Multiply By	To Get
Millimeters	0.0394	Inches
Centimeters	0.3937	Inches
Centimeters	0.0328	Feet
Meters	3.2808	Feet